Real

Reading 1

without answers

Liz Driscoll

D1331173

CAMBRIDGE
UNIVERSITY PRESS

CAMBRIDGE UNIVERSITY PRESS
Cambridge, New York, Melbourne, Madrid, Cape Town, Singapore, São Paulo, Delhi

Cambridge University Press
The Edinburgh Building, Cambridge CB2 8RU, UK

www.cambridge.org
Information on this title: www.cambridge.org/9780521702034

First published 2008
Reprinted 2008

Printed in the United Kingdom at the University Press, Cambridge

A catalogue record for this publication is available from the British Library

ISBN 978-0-521-70203-4

Contents

Map of the book

Unit number	Title	Topic	How to ...
1	We're here!	Airports and travel	o identify English words o follow signs and read notices at an airport o look at a website and find out the best way to travel on from an airport
2	What can I eat?	Food and eating out	o understand a text without knowing the meaning of every word o book breakfast in a hotel o choose food from a menu
3	Where will I find it?	Shopping	o scan a notice to find the information you need o find out when shops are open o read a store guide and find out where to buy things o read signs to understand them
4	Can I get money here?	Money	o buy money at a Currency Exchange and understand a leaflet about returning unused currency o predict the content of a text by thinking about the topic in your own language o follow instructions to use an ATM
5	Somewhere to stay	Hotels	o skim a hotel website and form an opinion of the hotel o find out details about a hotel's facilities o choose a suitable hotel
6	Is this what I need?	Health care and toiletries	o identify and find things in a chemist's o skim a text to find the part that is most useful to you o decide if medication is suitable o follow instructions on packets
7	Who's it from?	Keeping in touch	o work out the main purposes of cards o read a message aloud o understand a message on a card o identify types of messages o read a message and respond to it
8	Where can we park?	Parking	o find words with similar meanings in a text o try and work out the meaning of unknown words o read a leaflet about parking and work out where to park o find out about pay and display parking

Social and Travel

	Unit number	Title	Topic	How to ...
Social and Travel	9	Let's go there	Bergen	• find out what is available at a Tourist Information office • read a leaflet and find out when the attraction is open and how much it costs • use grammar to help link words in sentences
	10	I'd like to register	Health care	• find out how to register at a medical centre • find out how to see a doctor • put the sentences of a text into your own words • complete a health questionnaire
	11	What's on tonight?	Television and films	• use a dictionary with English definitions • read a TV guide and choose programmes to watch • read a film review and understand the writer's opinion
Work and Study	12	This school sounds good!	Choosing a school	• find out about a language school from its website • guess the meaning of new words from the context • choose a language course
	13	I've chosen this one!	Readers	• use the cover and blurb of a book to predict its type and topic • choose a reader • read whole sections of a story without stopping
	14	Use a pencil!	Exams	• read and understand a description of the KET exam • identify exam tasks • follow exam instructions and do the tasks
	15	It's on the noticeboard	Jobs and advertisements	• scan advertisements and find information • understand a list of tips • skim advertisements and decide if they are useful
	16	I'm working nights	In the workplace	• work out who and what pronouns and possessive adjectives refer to • find out about the duties of a job • understand a memo • identify duties that have not been carried out

Acknowledgements

I would like to thank Nóirín Burke and Ros Henderson, of Cambridge University Press for their support and guidance in the writing of this book. I am also grateful to Sue F Jones for her contribution to its editing, to Linda Matthews for its production, and to Stephanie White and Paul Fellows for its design.

My thanks also go to Ian Lees, Marcos Martos Higueras and Judy Shakespeare for their help in finding the texts.

The author and publishers are grateful to the following reviewers for their valuable insights and suggestions:

Steve Banfield, United Arab Emirates
Ildiko Berke, Hungary
Vanessa Boutefeu, Portugal
Ian Chisholm, United Kingdom
Alper Darici, Turkey
Rosie Ganne, United Kingdom
Jean Greenwood, United Kingdom
Elif Isler, Turkey
Kathy Kolarik, Australia
Ms L. Krishnaveni, Malaysia
Philip Lodge, United Arab Emirates
Steve Miller, United Kingdom
Ersoy Osman, United Kingdom

The authors and publishers acknowledge the following sources of copyright material and are grateful for the permissions granted. While every effort has been made, it has not always been possible to identify the sources of all the material used, or to trace all copyright holders. If any omissions are brought to our notice, we will be happy to include the appropriate acknowledgements on reprinting.

pp. 15–16: the text 'Breakfast' and 'Light Bites' from the Travelodge brochure, Travelodge; p. 23: the extract from 'Buy Back Plus' leaflet, Travelex UK Limited; pp. 26–27: the adapted extract from the Mercure Luxor hotel brochure, Accor Hotels, www.accorhotels.com; p. 28–29: the adapted text from hotel brochure, The Aladin Group www.nefertitihotel. com; pp. 30 and 32: the advertisement for Nurofen®, Reckitt Benckiser plc; p. 31: the till receipt from Boots, the Boots Logo is a trade mark of The Boots Company PLC; p. 33: the Vicks Sinex Decongestant Nasal Spray packet, Proctor and Gamble UK; p. 39: text adapted from 'Driving into Oxford made easy', Oxfordshire County Council, www.oxfordshire. gov.uk, © Crown Copyright; p. 40: notice on 'Pay and display machine', Oxford County Council, Environment and Economy, © Crown Copyright; pp. 43–45: extracts from the Bergen Tourist Guide 2006, Bergen Tourist Board; p. 56: the leaflet 'Discover Rotorua and Waitomo', Great Sights, www. greatsights.co.nz; p. 67: extract from A Picture to Remember by Sarah Scott-Malden, 1999, text from within pages 3-7, © Cambridge University Press reproduced with permission; p. 68: adapted extract from Objective KET Student's Book by Annette Capel and Wendy Sharp p. 6, © Cambridge University Press, reproduced with permission; p. 68 and pp. 70–71: the extracts from the Key English Test Reading and Writing Answer sheet, and extracts from Key English Text 1 examination papers, University of Cambridge ESOL Examinations for. Reproduced with the kind permission of Cambridge ESOL.

The publishers are grateful to the following for permission to reproduce copyright photographs and material:

Key: l = left, c = centre, r = right, t = top, b = bottom

Alamy/©Jeremy Horner for p. 41; Corbis Images/©Jose Fuste Raga for p. 26; Getty Images/©Image Bank for p. 27, /©Altrendo Images for p. 40, /©Taxi for p63; Ronald Grant Archive for pp. 52 (t) and 52 (b); The Kobal Collection/ ©Studio Ghibli for p. 52 (c); Nefertiti Hotel for p. 28; Photolibrary.com/©Vidler Vidler for p. 36; The Travel Library/ ©John Lawrence for p. 43, /©Roberta Matassa for p. 61.

Illustrations:

Kathy Baxendale pp. 13tr, 28; Mark Duffin pp. 11, 13l, 14, 18, 19, 20, 21, 24, 25, 30, 33, 34, 36tr, 58, 59, 72, 74, 79; Kamae Design p 40; Katie Mac p. 76; Laura Martinez p. 10b; Mark Watkinson p. 10t; Ian West p. 46.

Text design and page make-up: Kamae Design, Oxford
Cover design: Kamae Design, Oxford
Cover photo: © Getty
Picture research: Hilary Luckcock

Introduction
To the student

Who is *Real Reading 1* for?

You can use this book if you are a student at elementary level and you want to improve your English reading. You can use the book alone without a teacher or you can use it in a classroom with a teacher.

How will *Real Reading 1* help me with my reading?

Real Reading 1 contains texts for everyday reading practice, for example TV guides, leaflets, advertisements, maps, signs in shops and instructions on medication. It is designed to help you with reading you will need to do in English at home or when visiting another country.

The exercises in each unit help you develop useful skills such as working out the meaning of unknown words from context and ignoring parts of the text which are not useful to you. *Real Reading 1* discourages you from using a dictionary to find out the meaning of every word you don't know.

How is *Real Reading 1* organized?

The book has 16 units and is divided into two sections:
- Units 1–11 – social and travel situations
- Units 12–16 – work and study situations

Every unit is divided into Reading A and Reading B and has:
- *Get ready to read*: to introduce you to the topic of the unit
- *Learning tip*: to help you improve your learning
- *Class bonus*: an exercise you can do with other students or friends
- *Focus on*: to help you study useful grammar or vocabulary
- *Did you know?*: extra information about vocabulary, different cultures or the topic of the unit
- *Extra practice*: an extra exercise for more practice
- *Can-do checklist*: to help you think about what you learnt in the unit

After each section there is a review unit. The reviews help you practise the skills you learn in each section.

At the back of the book you can find:
- *Appendices*: contain lists of *Useful language*, *Learning tips* for every unit and information about *Using a dictionary*
- *Answer key* (only in self-study edition): gives correct answers and possible answers for exercises that have more than one answer

How can I use *Real Reading 1*?

The units at the end of the book are more difficult than the units at the beginning of the book. However, you do not need to do the units in order. It is better to choose the units that are most interesting for you and to do them in the order you prefer.

There are many different ways you can use this book. We suggest you work in this way:
- Look in the *Contents* list and find a unit that interests you.
- Prepare yourself for reading by working through the *Get ready to read* exercises.
- Look at *Appendix 1: Useful language* for the unit.
- Do the exercises in Reading A. Use the example answers to guide you. Put the *Learning tip* into practice (either in Reading A or Reading B).
- Do the exercises in Reading B.
- Check your answers either with your teacher or with the *Answer key*.
- If you want to do more work, do the *Extra practice* activity.
- At the end of the unit, think about what you learnt and complete the *Can-do checklist*.
- Look at the list of *Learning tips* in *Appendix 2* and decide which other tips you have used in the unit.

Introduction
To the teacher

What is *Cambridge English Skills*?

Real Reading 1 is one of 12 books in the *Cambridge English Skills* series. The series also contains *Real Writing* and *Real Listening & Speaking* books and offers skills training to students from elementary to advanced level. All the books are available in with-answers and without-answers editions.

Level	Book	Author
Elementary CEF: A2 Cambridge ESOL: KET NQF Skills for life: Entry 2	Real Reading 1 with answers	Liz Driscoll
	Real Reading 1 without answers	Liz Driscoll
	Real Writing 1 with answers and audio CD	Graham Palmer
	Real Writing 1 without answers	Graham Palmer
	Real Listening & Speaking 1 with answers and audio CDs (2)	Miles Craven
	Real Listening & Speaking 1 without answers	Miles Craven
Pre-intermediate CEF: B1 Cambridge ESOL: PET NQF Skills for life: Entry 3	Real Reading 2 with answers	Liz Driscoll
	Real Reading 2 without answers	Liz Driscoll
	Real Writing 2 with answers and audio CD	Graham Palmer
	Real Writing 2 without answers	Graham Palmer
	Real Listening & Speaking 2 with answers and audio CDs (2)	Sally Logan & Craig Thaine
	Real Listening & Speaking 2 without answers	Sally Logan & Craig Thaine
Intermediate to upper-intermediate CEF: B2 Cambridge ESOL: FCE NQF Skills for life: Level 1	Real Reading 3 with answers	Liz Driscoll
	Real Reading 3 without answers	Liz Driscoll
	Real Writing 3 with answers and audio CD	Roger Gower
	Real Writing 3 without answers	Roger Gower
	Real Listening & Speaking 3 with answers and audio CDs (2)	Miles Craven
	Real Listening & Speaking 3 without answers	Miles Craven
Advanced CEF: C1 Cambridge ESOL: CAE NQF Skills for life: Level 2	Real Reading 4 with answers	Liz Driscoll
	Real Reading 4 without answers	Liz Driscoll
	Real Writing 4 with answers and audio CD	Simon Haines
	Real Writing 4 without answers	Simon Haines
	Real Listening & Speaking 4 with answers and audio CDs (2)	Miles Craven
	Real Listening & Speaking 4 without answers	Miles Craven

Where are the teacher's notes?

The series is accompanied by a dedicated website containing detailed teaching notes and extension ideas for every unit of every book. Please visit www.cambridge.org/englishskills to access the *Cambridge English Skills* teacher's notes.

What are the main aims of *Real Reading 1*?

- To help students develop reading skills in accordance with the ALTE (Association of Language Testers in Europe) Can-do statements. These statements describe what language users can typically do at different levels and in different contexts. Visit www.alte.org for further information.
- To encourage autonomous learning by focusing on learner training.

What are the key features of *Real Reading 1*?

- It is aimed at elementary learners of English at level A2 of the Council of Europe's CEFR (Common European Framework of Reference for Languages).
- It contains 16 four-page units, divided into two sections: Social and Travel and Work and Study.
- *Real Reading 1* units are divided into Reading A and Reading B and contain:
  - *Get ready to read* warm-up exercises to get students thinking about the topic
  - *Learning tips* which give students advice on how to improve their reading and their learning
  - *Class bonus* communication activities for pairwork and group work so that you can adapt the material to suit your classes
  - *Focus on* exercises which provide contextualized practice in particular grammar or vocabulary areas
  - *Did you know?* boxes which provide notes on cultural or linguistic differences between English-speaking countries, or factual information on the topic of the unit
  - *Extra practice* extension tasks which provide more real world reading practice
  - *Can-do checklists* at the end of every unit to encourage students to think about what they have learnt
- There are two review units to practise skills that have been introduced in the units.
- It has an international feel and contains a range of texts from English-speaking and other countries.
- It can be used as self-study material, in class, or as supplementary homework material.

What is the best way to use *Real Reading 1* in the classroom?

The book is designed so that the units may be used in any order, although the more difficult units naturally appear near the end of the book, in the *Work and Study* section.

You can consult the unit-by-unit teacher's notes at www.cambridge.org/englishskills for detailed teaching ideas. However, broadly speaking, different parts of the book can be approached in the following ways:

- *Useful language*: You can use the *Useful language* lists in *Appendix 1* to preteach or revise the vocabulary from the unit you are working on.
- *Get ready to read*: It is a good idea to use this section as an introduction to the topic. Students can work on the exercises in pairs or groups. Many of these require students to answer questions about their personal experience. These questions can be used as prompts for discussion. Some exercises contain a problem-solving element that students can work on together. Other exercises aim to clarify key vocabulary in the unit. You can present these vocabulary items directly to students.
- *Learning tips*: You can ask students to read and discuss these in an open-class situation. An alternative approach is for you to create a series of discussion questions associated with the *Learning tip*. Students can discuss their ideas in pairs or small groups followed by open-class feedback. The *Learning tip* acts as a reflective learning tool to help promote learner autonomy.
- *Class bonuses*: The material in these activities aims to provide freer practice. You can set these up carefully, then take the role of observer during the activity so that students carry out the task freely. You can make yourself available to help students or to analyze the language they produce during the activity.
- *Extra practice*: These activities can be set as homework or out-of-class projects for your students. Alternatively, students can do some activities in pairs during class time.
- *Can-do checklists*: Refer to these at the beginning of a lesson to explain to students what the lesson will cover, and again at the end so that students can evaluate their learning for themselves.
- *Appendices*: You may find it useful to refer your students to the *Useful language, Learning tips* and *Using a dictionary* sections. Students can use these as general checklists to help them with their reading.

Unit 1
We're here!

Get ready to read

What are these different kinds of transport?

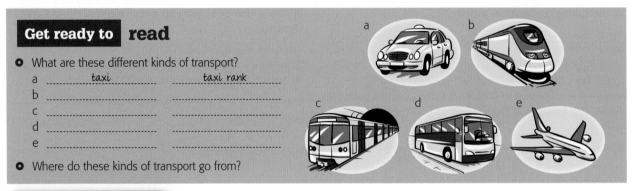

a ....taxi............ ....taxi rank............
b ....
c ....
d ....
e ....

● Where do these kinds of transport go from?

go to Useful language p. 82

A At the airport

1 Look at the pictures. What are the people doing? Match the sentences with the pictures.

a They're collecting their baggage. ☐ 3
b They're going through Customs. ☐
c They're showing their passports. ☐
d They're arriving at the airport. ☐

Did you know ...?

English is the international language of travel and communication. You will usually find information in the language of the country you are in – and in English. For example, at an airport in Spain, you may see this notice:
PASO AUTORIZADO SOLAMENTE PASAJEROS
PASSENGERS ONLY BEYOND THIS POINT

1

2

3

4

2 Look at the four groups of signs and notices below. Match them
   with the four pictures in Exercise 1.

Welcome to Oslo airport   A 1
Velkommen til Oslo Lufthavn

Camera surveillance
Kameraovervåketområde

No smoking
Røyking forbudt

Toilets
Toaletter

Baggage trolleys   B ☐
Bagasjetraller

Customs ↑   C ☐
Toll

Animals
Dyr

Goods to declare
Varer til fortolling

Nothing to declare
Intet å fortolle

All passports ↓   D ☐
Alle pass

Wait here
Vent her

EC/EEA citizens
EU/ES borgere

Learning tip

If you speak a European language, some English
words may look similar to words in your language.
This will help you to understand the meaning of
words you do not know. For example:
arrivals – *arrivi* (Italian)
passport – *pasaporte* (Spanish)
baggage – *bagages* (French)
passenger – *passageiro* (Portuguese)
toilet – *toaleta* (Polish)

3 Look at the airport signs and notices in
   Exercises 1 and 2 again. Which words are in
   English? ....

4 Do you know which language the other words
   are in? Is there a clue in one of the notices in
   Exercise 2? ....

5 Are any of the words in the signs and notices
   the same in both languages? Which words are
   similar? ....

6 Look at the English signs and notices again.
   Are any of the words similar in your language?

Focus on ...
vocabulary

There are many useful words in this section
about airports and travel. Read the descriptions
of some of the words. Write each word.

a someone who is travelling in a car, aeroplane, etc.,
   but not controlling the car, aeroplane, etc.
   p a s s e n g e r

b a metal structure on wheels which is used for carrying
   things _ _ _ _ _ _ _

c a small book with your photograph in that you need
   to enter a country _ _ _ _ _ _ _ _

d all the suitcases and bags that you take with you
   when you travel _ _ _ _ _ _ _

e the area where someone examines your bags when
   you are going into a country _ _ _ _ _ _ _

f we say this to someone who has just arrived
   _ _ _ _ _ _ _

E✗tra practice

Where can you find English signs and notices in your
country? Start a list of English words you see in your town
or city.

B Getting into the city

1 Imagine you are going to Oslo for four days and you are staying in a hotel in the city centre. Before you leave home, you want to find out how to get to the city centre. What would you do? Tick ✓ one or more of the boxes.

    a I'd look in a guidebook. ☐
    b I'd ask someone who knows the place. ☐
    c I'd look on the Internet. ☐
    d I'd ask at a travel agent's. ☐

2 Your friend went to Oslo last year. Read what she told you about transport into the city centre. Does anything she said surprise you?

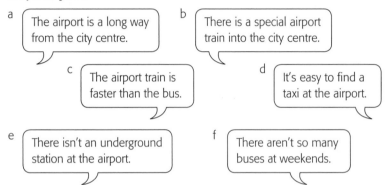

a The airport is a long way from the city centre.

b There is a special airport train into the city centre.

c The airport train is faster than the bus.

d It's easy to find a taxi at the airport.

e There isn't an underground station at the airport.

f There aren't so many buses at weekends.

3 Look quickly at the text below. Where is the text from?

4 Read what your friend told you in Exercise 2 again. <u>Underline</u> the information in the website which confirms what she said.

Class bonus

Write six true/false sentences about the airport guide. Exchange your sentences with a partner. Are your friend's sentences true or false?

It takes 20 minutes to get to the city centre on the special airport train.

E ✗ tra practice

Look at the website again. Look at the words in *italics*. They are places in the centre of Oslo. What are their names in English? Can you work them out?

http://www.osl.no/

OSL⊕ AIRPORT

AIRPORT GUIDE
➔ Location

Oslo Gardermoen airport is 50 km (31 miles) north of Oslo city.

Public transport into Oslo

TRAIN: The Airport Express Train (Flytoget) is the quickest way (journey time: 20 minutes) into the city centre. Some Flytoget trains run between the airport and Oslo *Sentralstasjon* only. Others also stop at underground stations, including the main underground station *Nationaltheatret*. A single ticket costs 180 kroner. All inter-city and express trains from Skien, Lillehammer and Trondheim also stop at Oslo Airport Gardermoen station on their way to Oslo. These trains are cheaper, but not as frequent.

TAXI: There are always taxis at the airport terminal; if you have a wheelchair, you can arrange a taxi through Airport Taxis (tel: 23 232 323). There is a taxi information desk in the Arrivals hall and the taxi rank is outside Arrivals.

BUS: The SAS Airport Bus (Flybussen) runs between Oslo Airport Gardermoen and Oslo *Bussterminalen* and continues to the Radisson Scandinavia Hotel (journey time: 40 minutes). The first stop is Furuset skole and you can get on the underground here. The bus leaves every 20 minutes on weekdays, and every 20-30 minutes at weekends. The last bus leaves the airport at 01.00.

COACH: The airport coach *NOR-WAY Bussekspress* runs to/from Oslo, Bærum, Fredrikstad and Gjøvik.

5 Look at the address of your hotel and the map of central Oslo. Find the hotel and three of the places from the website on the map. Which place is nearest to your hotel?

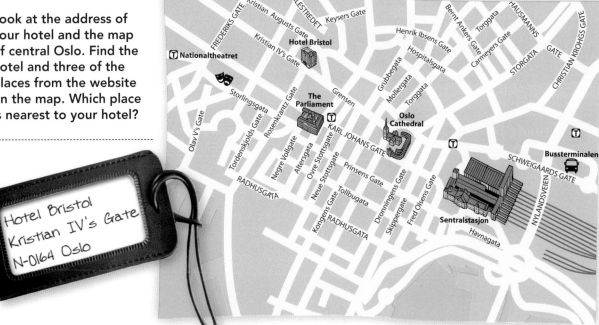

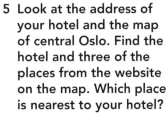

Hotel Bristol
Kristian IV's Gate
N-0164 Oslo

6 Look at the ticket and timetable. Circle the correct word.

a The *ticket* / *timetable* is for the train.
b The *ticket* / *timetable* is for the bus.

```
10648865/032966 0015895

SAS  Flybussen
       Org.nr. 986 978 364 MVA
                  09.08.07 14:34
       SL Ovg. gyldig til 16:24
---------------------------------
FRA: Oslo Lufthavn
TIL: Oslo City

1 Voksen          120
      SUM: Kr.120

Herav 8% mva Kr.17,78
Gr.lag Kr. 222,22

www.flybussen.no
```

From Oslo Airport
Valid from 11th June 2006

	Oslo Airport Gardermoen	Lillestrøm	Oslo Central Station	Nationaltheatret	Skøyen	Lysaker	Sandvika	Asker
First departure	0536	0548	0558	0603	0608	0610	0618	0624
	46*		05*					
	56	08	18	23	28	30	38	44
Minutes past every hour	06*		25*					
	16	28	43	43	48	50	58	04
	26*		45*					
	36	48	58	03	08	10	18	24
Final departure	0036	0048	0058	0103	0108	0110	0118	0124

*Departures every 10 minutes Monday–Friday 0646–2246, Sundays 1246–2346. Saturdays and the period 9th July–6th August departures every 20 minutes. Subject to alteration on public holidays.
See www.flytoget.no or call + 47 815 00 777.

7 Look at the ticket, the timetable and the website again. Answer these questions.

a How often are the trains / buses?

b How much does the train / bus cost?

8 How would you travel to your hotel in the centre of Oslo?

I'd travel

E**✗**tra practice

Which airport is nearest to your home? Look on the Internet and find some information in English about transport to/from this airport. Write sentences like the sentences in Exercise 2.

Can-do checklist

Tick what you can do.

	Can do	Need more practice
I can identify English words.	✓	✓
I can follow signs and read notices at an airport.		
I can look at a website and find out the best way to travel on from an airport.	✓	

Unit2
What can I eat?

Get ready to read

○ Circle the words so that the sentences are true for you.
  I eat *two / three / more than three* meals a day.
  My favourite meal of the day is *breakfast / lunch / dinner*.
  I usually eat *with my family / with my friends / on my own*.
  I *never / sometimes / often* eat out.

○ Look at the food and drink. Circle the correct word in each pair.
  a *noodles / rice*
  b *beans / tomatoes*
  c *coffee / soup*
  d *mushrooms / potatoes*
  e *jam / toast*
  f *cereal / juice*
  g *a banana / a croissant*
  h *butter / eggs*

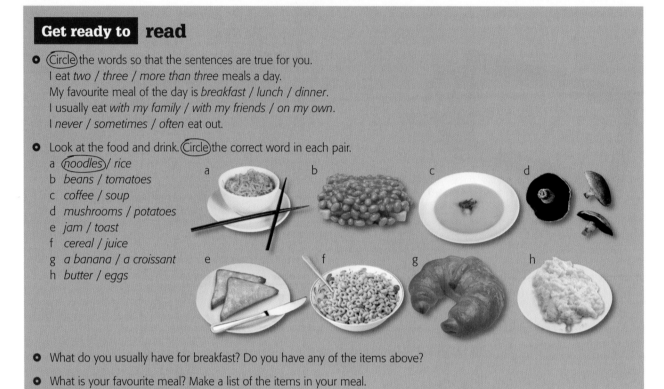

○ What do you usually have for breakfast? Do you have any of the items above?

○ What is your favourite meal? Make a list of the items in your meal.

go to Useful language p. 82

A The most important meal of the day

1 **Look at the text on the opposite page quickly. Answer these questions. Tick ✓ one of the boxes.**

  a What is it?
     a menu ☐
     a leaflet ☐
     a bill ☐
  b Where is it from?
     a café ☐
     a shop ☐
     a hotel ☐

2 **Look at the photographs on the opposite page. Which of the items in *Get ready to read* can you see?**

Learning tip

When you read, it is not necessary to understand every word in the text. You only need to understand the parts of the text which contain the information you are looking for.

3 **What does the leaflet call the two types of breakfast in the photographs?**

----

4 **You're interested in having breakfast in the hotel. Read the leaflet again and complete the chart.**

	full breakfast	breakfast bag
a When can you have breakfast?		any time
b Where can you have it?		
c How much does it cost?		
d Where and when do you pay?		

breakfast

All you can eat for just £6.50.*

Relax with a tasty full breakfast from our breakfast buffet ...

& kids eat free!**

Help yourself to breakfast between 7am—10am (8am—11am at weekends)

Just book and pay at reception when you check in.

*Price of breakfast includes only items served from the breakfast buffet, including tea, coffee and juice.
**Kids eat free offer applies to children 10 years or under and applies to up to two 'kids' per paying adult only.

The most important meal of the day...

Breakfast in your room or on the run for only £4.

Getting up early, pressed for time or got an attack of the midnight munchies?

Why not try our breakfast bag? Enjoy it in your room or take it on your journey. You can order one from reception any time or if you order before you go to bed, we can deliver one to your door for the next morning.***

***we will deliver to your door between 5am and 7am only. Breakfast bags can only be purchased from reception. Pictures of food are for illustrative purposes only. Actual dishes may differ.

Did you know ...?

The most famous meal in Britain used to be the traditional fried breakfast. Nowadays people usually only eat a cooked breakfast in hotels or cafés. In general, people don't eat so much meat, and also they are always in a hurry in the morning. The most popular breakfast is cereal or toast.

5 The leaflet mentions *breakfast buffet*. Do you think this means that there is waiter service or is it self-service? Find two words in the leaflet which give the answer.

Class bonus

Close your books. Write a list of breakfast items in the photographs. The winner is the student who remembers the most items!

B Here's the menu

1 Look at the menu below quickly. Answer these questions with *yes* or *no*.

a   Is this a menu for a vegetarian restaurant?   ...*no*...
b   Does the menu show food and drinks?   ....
c   Does it show prices?   ....
d   Are there any desserts on the menu?   ....

2 Look at the menu carefully. Which food items do the dishes contain? Make three lists in your notebook, like this:

MEAT	VEGETABLES	OTHER
chicken	salad	cheese

3 You now know enough to choose your meal from the menu. What would you choose? Why?

I'd choose ....

MENU

appetisers

Goat's cheese salad ⓥ   £3.75
Soft cheese on a mixed salad.

Thai chicken   £3.25
Tender chicken pieces served with a sweet Thai sauce.

Soup of the day ⓥ   £2.95
Ask a member of staff for today's soup. Served with a bread roll & butter.

mains

Fish & chips   £6.50
Fried cod served with chunky chips & peas.

Sausage & mash   £6.50
Tasty beef sausage served with mashed potato, peas & a light gravy.

Chicken salad with grapes   £6.75
Sliced chicken breast & grapes served on a mixed salad.

6oz (170g) steak   £7.95
Sirloin steak served with chunky chips, peas, tomatoes & onion rings.

Cheese and onion tart ⓥ   £6.95
Served with a mixed salad.

Cheeseburger ⓓ   £5.95
Served with chunky chips & a mixed salad.

ⓓ **Make it a double burger for just £1 extra.**

ⓥ **Suitable for vegetarians.**

4 Look at the text in *italics* on the menu. The text in *italics* describes the dish. Find the word or words which answer these questions.

a Goat's cheese salad – what kind of cheese?

  soft cheese

b Thai chicken – what kind of chicken?

c Thai chicken – what exactly is Thai in this dish?

d Fish & chips – what kind of fish?

e Fish & chips – what kind of chips?

f Sausage & mash – what kind of sausage?

g Chicken salad with grapes – what kind of chicken?

h 6oz (170g) steak – what kind of steak?

Focus on ...
vocabulary

Circle the word in each pair which matches the short definition.

a a liquid which goes with food   pieces / sauce
b a cut of meat   breast / sirloin
c an adjective meaning 'big'   chunky / soft
d food can be cut this way   fried / sliced
e easy to cut   tasty / tender

Write each unused word above next to the correct definition.

f a part of the body   ....
g an adjective meaning 'nice'   ....
h food can be cooked in this way   ....
i opposite of hard   ....
j small bits   _pieces_

5 Imagine you are at the restaurant with a group of friends. What would you recommend to the following people?

For someone who	I'd recommend	followed by
a is vegetarian		
b doesn't like salad		
c loves cheese		
d is on a diet		

Class bonus

Make a class menu. Choose a dish. Then write a one-line description of it (like the *italics* on the menu). Then look at the menu and choose from other students' dishes.

E X tra practice

Have you ever seen a menu in your country which is both in your language and in English? The next time you see a menu in English, try and work out what the dishes are.

Can-do checklist

Tick what you can do.

	Can do	Need more practice
I can understand a text without knowing the meaning of every word.	✓	✓
I can book breakfast in a hotel.		
I can choose food from a menu.		

Unit 3
Where will I find it?

Get ready to read

- Write the names of the things in the list on the left. Which shop would you go to in your town or city if you wanted to buy these things?

  a .... DVD ....   ----------------------------------

  b ----------------------   ----------------------------------

  c ----------------------   ----------------------------------

  d ----------------------   ----------------------------------

  e ---------------------- ,   ----------------------------------

  f ----------------------   ----------------------------------

- Are these specialist shops or department stores? Write *S* or *D* after the name of the shop.

go to Useful language p. 83

a   b   c   d   f   DICTIONARY   e

A It's on the ground floor

Learning tip

Scanning is when we read a text quickly to find a particular piece of information. We do not read every word. We stop reading when we find the information we want.

1 Three people want to go to three different shops. Match their questions with what they are thinking.

1   Is it open on Sundays?   [c]

2   What time does it open in the mornings?   [ ]

3   Is it open late one evening?   [ ]

a   Perhaps I can go before I go to school.

b   I finish work at six o'clock, but I could go on my way home.

c   I can't go during the week, but I could go at the weekend.

2 Now look at the shop opening hours. Find the answers to the questions. (question 1 = text 1, question 2 = text 2, question 3 = text 3.)

1   Yes, it is. It's open from 11am to 5pm on Sundays.

2   --

3   --

1

HMV records

Monday	08.30 – 6.30
Tuesday	08.30 – 6.30
Wednesday	08.30 – 6.30
Thursday	08.30 – 7.00
Friday	08.30 – 6.30
Saturday	08.30 – 6.30
Sunday	11.00 – 5.00

2

Sainsbury's supermarket

We're open

Monday–Saturday
7am–11pm
Sunday
11am–5pm

3

DEBENHAMS department store

Monday	9.00	to	18.00
Tuesday	9.00	to	18.00
Wednesday	9.00	to	20.00
Thursday	9.00	to	18.00
Friday	9.00	to	18.00
Saturday	9.00	to	18.00
Sunday	11.00	to	17.00

This store is air conditioned.
This is a no-smoking environment.
No dogs except guide dogs.

3 You go to Debenhams on Wednesday evening. You are looking for these things. Match the things with what the shop assistant says.

a Ties are in Men's accessories. [6]

b You'll find perfume in Cosmetics. ☐

c Boots are in Women's footwear. ☐

d Baby clothes are in Childrenswear. ☐

e You'll find suitcases in Luggage. ☐

f Mobile phones are in Gadgets and games. ☐

Did you know …?

GB English	US English
ground floor	first floor
first floor	second floor
second floor	third floor

4 Scan the store guide. On which floor will you find the departments in Exercise 3?

a Men's accessories   ground floor
b Cosmetics   ....
c Women's footwear   ....
d Childrenswear   ....
e Luggage   ....
f Gadgets and games   ....

Class bonus

Write a list of six things you want to buy in the department store. Give your list to a partner. Find the department and floor for your partner's six things.

5 Scan the store guide again and find the answers to these questions. Which floor do you need to go to?

a Can I make a phone call?
  Yes, you can. There's a telephone on the first floor.
b Are there any toilets?
  ----
c Can I get some money here?
  ----
d Do they repair shoes?
  ----
e Can I have something to eat?
  ----
f Is there a hairdresser's?

STORE GUIDE

2 Childrenswear
  Children's accessories
  Home
  Luggage

1 Account opening/
  payments
  Baby facilities
  Collect by car
  Disabled facilities
  Ordering service
  Restaurant
  Telephone
  Toilets
  Wedding service
  Womenswear

G Account opening/
  payments
  Café
  Cash machine
  Ordering service
  Personal shopper
  Watch repairs

  Accessories
  Cosmetics
  Gadgets and games
  Jewellery and watches
  Menswear
  Men's accessories
  Men's footwear
  Women's accessories
  Women's footwear

Focus on …
spelling

One word in each pair is spelled incorrectly. Circle the correct spelling. Then check your answers in the store guide.

a (accessories)   acessories
b restarant   restaurant
c telephon   telephone
d gadgets   gadjets
e jewellery   jewelery
f machine   mashine

B What does that sign say?

1 You are in a department store and you want to do these things. Which sign should you look for? Match the signs with the things you want to do.

a You want to try on a pair of trousers. ☑3
b You want to have a cup of coffee. ☐
c You want to go up to the second floor. ☐
d You want to order a smaller pair of trousers. ☐
e You want to leave the building. ☐
f You want to pay. ☐

2 While you are looking for the signs in Exercise 1, you see the signs below. Look at each sign and answer the question.

FIRE EXIT ONLY
This door will open in an emergency

a Can you get out here?
  No, you can't. (You can only get out when there's a fire.)

BUY 1 GET 1 HALF PRICE
on hundreds of best-selling CDs

d Does this mean you get two CDs for the price of one?

TAX FREE SHOPPING
for non-EC residents
When you spend a minimum of £50*
*excludes childrenswear
Ask any sales assistant for details

b Can everyone have tax free shopping?

LIFT OUT OF ORDER

e Can I go up to the second floor in the lift?

SALE STARTS TODAY!
Up to 30% off our original prices

c Do things cost less than usual?

Shoes repaired while you wait

f Must I come back later for my shoes?
----

3 Look at these notices on shop windows and doors. Match the notices with the explanations below.

a You can shop here six days a week. ☑
b The shop is open one evening. ☐
c You mustn't eat anything in this shop. ☐
d Be careful when you come through the door. ☐
e You can't get out here. ☐
f You must pay in cash. ☐

1 We do not accept cheques or credit cards

4 Please use other door

2 Open daily 10 - 6 (except Mondays)

5 Mind your head

3 Late night shopping Thursdays – till 8pm

6 No food in this shop, please

4 Look at these notices. Explain them in your own words.

a OPEN WEEKDAYS ONLY

b Sorry – no cash

c Fire door Keep closed

d All this week Buy 2 get 1 free

e No bicycles against this window

f All towels – 25% cheaper

E X tra practice

Go into a shop or department store in your town. Look at the signs and notices. How do you say these things in English? Rewrite the signs and notices.

Can-do checklist

Tick what you can do.

	Can do	Need more practice
I can scan a notice to find the information I need.	✔	✔
I can find out when shops are open.		
I can read a store guide and find out where to buy things.		
I can read signs to understand them.		

Unit 4
Can I get money here?

go to Useful language p. 83

Get ready to read

⊙ Where can you get foreign currency if you're going abroad? Tick ✓ the boxes.

	in your country before you go	in the country you're visiting
a at a Currency Exchange		
b at an ATM		
c at a bank		

⊙ Who asks these questions at a Currency Exchange – the customer (C) or the assistant (A)?

a Can I pay by *debit card* or *credit card*? ☐ C
b What's the *exchange rate*? ☐
c Can I see your *passport*? ☐
d Would you like *cash* or *travellers cheques*? ☐
e How much *commission* do you charge? ☐
f Can I have a *receipt*? ☐

⊙ Complete these sentences about using an ATM with the words in *italics*.

g You can use your _____debit card_____ or .... in an ATM.
h You don't need a .... to use an ATM.
i You can only get .... from an ATM – you can't get ....
j You can get a .... , which shows how much money you got.
k You don't know how much .... you have paid when you use an ATM. You only find out from your bank or credit card statement.
l You don't know the .... either. You only find out from your bank or credit card statement.

A Buy Back Plus

1 Mieko is on her way to Mexico City. She has just spent a few days in the United States. She is changing US dollars into Mexican pesos at Travelex at Los Angeles airport. Look at the leaflet on the opposite page quickly and answer her question.

> Can I return any Mexican pesos I don't spend?

> ....

2 Here are some more of Mieko's questions. Answer the questions with *yes* or *no*.

a
> Do I have to pay commission when I return pesos I haven't spent?

............*no*............

b
> When I return unspent pesos, is the exchange rate higher than for buying them?

....

c
> Do I have to pay for the Buy Back Plus offer?

....

d
> Is there a time limit on the Buy Back Plus offer?

....

3 Now answer the questions in Exercise 2 again. Give more details from the leaflet.

a No, it's commission free. ....
b ....
c ....
d ....

Buy Back Plus
Total peace of mind

Why take Buy Back Plus

GUARANTEED PEACE OF MIND

If you are returning from your journey within 31 days, we will buy back your foreign currency and travellers cheques:

• **Commission Free**

• **At the Original Exchange Rate you bought it**

Secure the value of your currency for your own peace of mind for only $5.

Commission Free

Terms & Conditions
• Offer available to Travelex customers exchanging in the USA only.
• Offer is non-transferable and subject to production of a valid passport.
• The purchase of cash and the purchase of Travellers Cheques are regarded as two separate exchanges even if purchased during the same visit.
• Maximum exchange limit of $10,000 applies.
• 'Buy Back Plus' exchanges must be completed within 31 days of the original purchase.
• Offer conditional on presentation of the original receipt and passport when returning foreign currency or travellers cheques.
• Offer valid for one return exchange only.
• Travelex will only buy back unspent currency bought from Travelex.
• Travelex reserves the right to withdraw Travelex 'Buy Back Plus' without any prior notice.

www.travelex.us Travelex worldwide money

4 Read the *Terms & Conditions* section of the leaflet. Are these sentences true (T) or false (F)?

a You can return your money to Travelex in the country you're going to. ..F..

b You have to pay $10 if you want to buy cash and travellers cheques at the same time. ....

c You can't return unspent currency more than a month after buying it. ....

d You must show your passport when returning your foreign currency. ....

e You can't return more foreign currency than you bought from Travelex. ....

5 Circle the correct verb to complete each sentence.

a You *must* / *don't have to* show your passport when exchanging money.

b You *can* / *can't* use the Buy Back Plus offer when exchanging more than $10,000.

c You *must* / *don't have to* show your receipt if you want to return your foreign currency.

d You *must* / *don't have to* return all your unspent currency at the same time.

e You *can* / *might not* always find this offer at Travelex in the USA.

6 Read the three sentences about Mieko's trip. Do you think she will use the Buy Back Plus offer? Why? / Why not?

a She wants to exchange $27 into Mexican pesos.

a *I don't think Mieko will use the Buy Back Plus offer because the cost of taking up the offer is $5 which is quite a large percentage of the $27 which she can return.*

b She's doing a two-month Spanish course in Mexico.

c She's only changing planes at Los Angeles on her way back to Tokyo.

7 Would you use the Travelex Buy Back Plus offer if you were going to a foreign country? Why? / Why not?

B Please insert your card

1 Mieko has just arrived in Mexico. She is going to get some money from an ATM. Tick ✓ the thing she needs to know before she uses the machine.

a her debit card number ☐
b her bank account number ☐
c her PIN (personal identification number) ☐

2 Which of these options do you have when you use an ATM in your country? Tick ✓ your answers.

a You can order a bank statement. ☐
b You can find out how much money you have in your bank account. ☐
c You can get money from the machine. ☐
d You can get a receipt. ☐
e You can order a cheque book. ☐
f You can start again if you make a mistake. ☐

3 Look at the nine screens. These show English instructions for using an ATM in Mexico. As you read the instructions, mime the actions and press the keys.

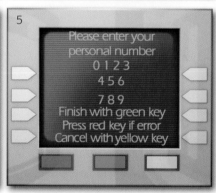

4 Which of the things in Exercise 2 can Mieko do at the Mexican ATM?

Did you know ...?

The first ATM was at Barclays Bank in Enfield, London. It was installed in 1967. The maximum withdrawal allowed was £10.

Focus on ...
verbs

There are seven verbs on the screens. These are the imperative form of the verb. (The imperative form is the same as the infinitive without 'to'.) We use the imperative form for instructions.
Complete the verbs.

a i n s e r t
b w _ _ _
c e _ _ _ _
d f _ _ _ _ _
e p _ _ _ _
f c _ _ _ _ _
g t _ _ _

Here are some instructions for a machine which you can use to change euros to dollars. Complete the instructions with some the verbs above.

h E _ _ _ _ _ the amount in figures.
i P _ _ _ _ _ C to cancel or change the amount.
j I _ _ _ _ _ _ your euro banknotes.
k T _ _ _ your US dollars.
l W _ _ _ for your receipt.

5 Look at the screen below. When might you see this screen on the ATM? Tick ✓ your answers.
1 after screen 1 ☐
2 after screen 2 ☐
3 after screen 3 ☐
4 after screen 4 ☐
5 after screen 5 ☐

You have not responded within the required time
Do you want to continue?

Yes   No

6 Look at screens 4 and 5 on the opposite page. Which buttons can you press on these screens if you don't want to continue?

Class bonus

Mieko decided not to continue. How many different ways can you finish this sentence?
'She decided not to continue because ...'

E✗tra practice

Next time you use an ATM, choose English instructions and follow them.

Can-do checklist

Tick what you can do.

	Can do	Need more practice
I can buy money at a Currency Exchange and understand a leaflet about returning unused currency.		
I can predict the content of a text by thinking about the topic in my own language.		
I can follow instructions to use an ATM.		

Unit 5
Somewhere to stay

go to Useful language p. 83

Get ready to read

- Tick ✓ the sentences which are true for you.
  I like to travel abroad on holiday. ☐
  I always go on organised holidays. ☐
  I usually go on holiday with my family. ☐
  I sometimes book holidays on the Internet. ☐
  I would like to travel round the world. ☐
  I like small family-run hotels. ☐

- This unit is about holidays in Egypt. Circle the correct words to make true sentences about Egypt.
  a   You can sail down the River *Amazon* / *Nile*.
  b   You can ride *a camel* / *an elephant*.
  c   You can visit pyramids, tombs and *castles* / *temples*.
  d   You can visit the cities of Cairo, Alexandria and *Luxor* / *Marrakech*.

A In the heart of the city

Learning tip

Skimming is when we read a text quickly to find out what it is about or to get a general idea. We do not read every word. We get the main idea and we don't pay attention to details. (See also *Learning tip* in Unit 6.)

1 Valeria and her sister are going on a week's holiday to Luxor. Valeria is checking the website of their hotel. Look at the words below. Skim the homepage. Circle the words which best describe the hotel.

   a   cheap / expensive
   b   big / small

2 Circle the words on the homepage which make you think that the Mercure Luxor is a top-class hotel.

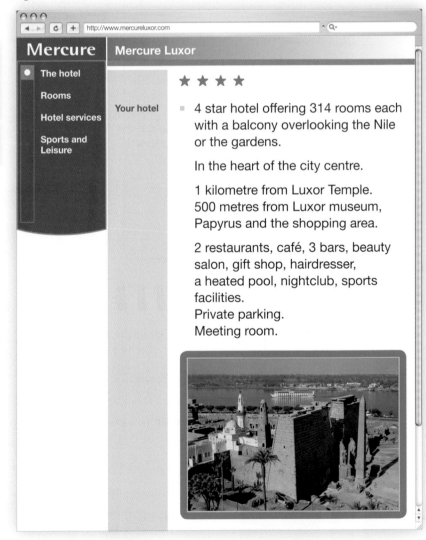

Mercure — Mercure Luxor

- The hotel
- Rooms
- Hotel services
- Sports and Leisure

Your hotel

★ ★ ★ ★

- 4 star hotel offering 314 rooms each with a balcony overlooking the Nile or the gardens.

  In the heart of the city centre.

  1 kilometre from Luxor Temple.
  500 metres from Luxor museum, Papyrus and the shopping area.

  2 restaurants, café, 3 bars, beauty salon, gift shop, hairdresser, a heated pool, nightclub, sports facilities.
  Private parking.
  Meeting room.

3 Think of five things you would expect to find in the bedroom of a top-class hotel. Read this webpage. Does it mention the things you thought of?

4 Look at the webpage again. What do you like most about the rooms?

> ### Focus on ...  compound nouns
>
> A compound noun is made up of two words – *art gallery*, for example. Find compound nouns on the webpages in this section which begin with these words: *city beauty gift air colour bath*

5 Valeria's sister has some questions about the hotel. Look at her questions. Answer the questions with *yes* or *no*.

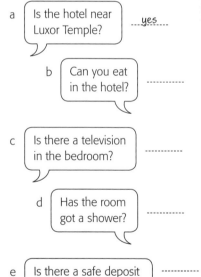

a Is the hotel near Luxor Temple? ....*yes*....

b Can you eat in the hotel? ....

c Is there a television in the bedroom? ....

d Has the room got a shower? ....

e Is there a safe deposit box in the bedroom? ....

6 Now answer the questions in Exercise 5 again. Give more details from the website.

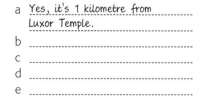

a Yes, it's 1 kilometre from Luxor Temple.

b ....

c ....

d ....

e ....

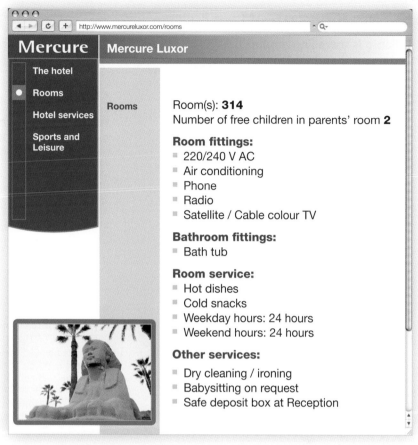

http://www.mercureluxor.com/rooms

Mercure | **Mercure Luxor**

The hotel
● Rooms
Hotel services
Sports and Leisure

Rooms

Room(s): **314**
Number of free children in parents' room **2**

Room fittings:
- 220/240 V AC
- Air conditioning
- Phone
- Radio
- Satellite / Cable colour TV

Bathroom fittings:
- Bath tub

Room service:
- Hot dishes
- Cold snacks
- Weekday hours: 24 hours
- Weekend hours: 24 hours

Other services:
- Dry cleaning / ironing
- Babysitting on request
- Safe deposit box at Reception

7 Here are some more questions. Can you find the answers to these questions on the website? Write *I don't know* if there is no information.

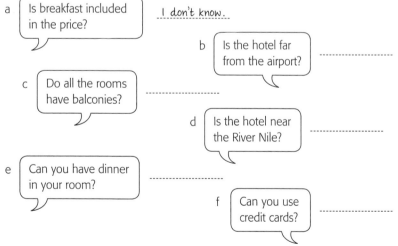

a Is breakfast included in the price? *I don't know.*

b Is the hotel far from the airport? ....

c Do all the rooms have balconies? ....

d Is the hotel near the River Nile? ....

e Can you have dinner in your room? ....

f Can you use credit cards? ....

8 Would you like to stay at the Mercure Luxor? Why? / Why not?

I'd like / I wouldn't like to stay at the Mercure Luxor because ....

> ### Class bonus
>
> Write six more questions about the hotel. Give your questions to a partner. Answer your partner's questions.

B This looks great!

1 Fabio is travelling around the world and is planning to travel to Luxor by train. Do you think the Mercure Luxor is a good hotel for him? Why? / Why not?

I think / I don't think the
Mercure Luxor is a good hotel
for Fabio because
....

2 Here are three questions Fabio always asks before he chooses a place to stay. Add two more questions to this list.

a Has my room got its own bathroom?

b Can I use the Internet?

c Is there a laundry service?

....
....
....
....

3 Look at three pages from the website for the Nefertiti Hotel. Write the answers to the three questions in Exercise 2.

a Yes, it has.

b ....

c ....

Did you know ...?

Nefertiti was a queen of Egypt who ruled from 1372–1350 BC. She was the wife of Akhenaton.

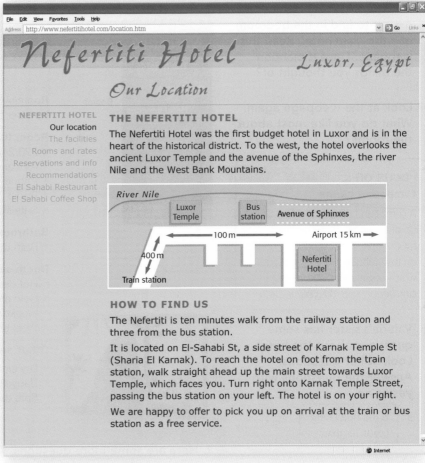

Nefertiti Hotel
Luxor, Egypt
Our Location

NEFERTITI HOTEL
Our location
The facilities
Rooms and rates
Reservations and info
Recommendations
El Sahabi Restaurant
El Sahabi Coffee Shop

THE NEFERTITI HOTEL

The Nefertiti Hotel was the first budget hotel in Luxor and is in the heart of the historical district. To the west, the hotel overlooks the ancient Luxor Temple and the avenue of the Sphinxes, the river Nile and the West Bank Mountains.

River Nile · Luxor Temple · Bus station · Avenue of Sphinxes · 100 m · Airport 15 km · 400 m · Nefertiti Hotel · Train station

HOW TO FIND US

The Nefertiti is ten minutes walk from the railway station and three from the bus station.

It is located on El-Sahabi St, a side street of Karnak Temple St (Sharia El Karnak). To reach the hotel on foot from the train station, walk straight ahead up the main street towards Luxor Temple, which faces you. Turn right onto Karnak Temple Street, passing the bus station on your left. The hotel is on your right.

We are happy to offer to pick you up on arrival at the train or bus station as a free service.

Nefertiti Hotel
Luxor, Egypt
The Facilities

NEFERTITI HOTEL
Our location
The facilities
Rooms and rates
Reservations and info
Recommendations
El Sahabi Restaurant
El Sahabi Coffee Shop

THE ROOF TERRACE

Our roof terrace is where you can relax and enjoy the fantastic panoramic view. We serve a variety of drinks and Egyptian dishes, and you can also order one of many different fruit sheeshas.

FREE SERVICES

For our guests, we provide free luggage storage and showers after checkout. Brochures and maps are available at the front desk. As always, we offer friendly and helpful service.

We also have:

- Satellite TV in the public rooms
- Internet service
- Laundry service
- Bike rentals
- Transportation
- Room service
- Souvenir shop
- Billiard table and games

4 Look at the webpages again. Answer these questions with *yes*, *no*, or *I don't know*. Write more details if you can.

a Is the hotel near Luxor Temple?

Yes, it's about 100 metres away

b Can you eat in the hotel?

----

c Is there a television in the bedroom?

----

d Has the room got a shower?

----

e Is there a safe deposit box in the bedroom?

----

f Is there a shop?

----

g Is breakfast included in the price?

----

h Is the hotel far from the airport?

----

i Do all the rooms have balconies?

----

j Is the hotel near the River Nile?

----

k Can you have dinner in your room?

----

l Can you use credit cards?

Address http://www.nefertitihotel.com/rates.htm

Nefertiti Hotel *Luxor, Egypt*

Rooms and Rates

NEFERTITI HOTEL
Our location
The facilities
Rooms and rates
Reservations and info
Recommendations
El Sahabi Restaurant
El Sahabi Coffee Shop

The Nefertiti has 25 rooms, all with air-conditioning, private shower and toilet.

Many rooms have balconies. We provide towels, toilet paper and soap.

	UK Sterling	Euros	US Dollar
Single	£5	€6	$7
Double	£7	€9	$11
Triple	£9	€12	$14

Also payable in Egyptian pounds.

Our healthy breakfasts are available anytime until noon (included with the room). You have your choice for a Continental or Egyptian breakfast.

5 Would you like to stay at the Nefertiti? Why? / Why not? Would you rather stay here or at the Mercure Luxor?

E **X** tra practice

Look on the Internet and find a website about a hotel in your country. Find some information in English. Do you think visitors will like this hotel?

Can-do checklist

Tick what you can do.

	Can do	Need more practice
I can skim a hotel website and form an opinion of the hotel.		
I can find out details about a hotel's facilities.		
I can choose a suitable hotel.		

Unit 6

Is this what I need?

Get ready to read

- Tick ✓ the things you can do at a chemist's in your country.
  - You can get tablets and medication. ☐
  - You can buy soap and shampoo. ☐
  - You can buy healthy food. ☐
  - You can get advice from the pharmacist. ☐
  - You can buy cosmetics. ☐
  - You can buy dental products. ☐

- Imagine you are on holiday and you have left your wash bag at home. What would you need to buy? Make a list.
  toothbrush, toothpaste, ...
  ....
  ....

go to Useful language p. 83 to p. 84

A I've forgotten my toothpaste

1 Look at the things in the pictures. Look at each label and circle the product.

1

MINT
MOUTHWASH
for healthy gums
250ml e

2
SKIN CARE
BODY LOTION
gives essential moisture from top to toe

3

STAY FRESH
Anti-Perspirant
total protection

4

HEADSTART
frequent use shampoo for normal hair

7

RISE n SHINE
SHOWER GEL
a fresh start for a fresh day

5
PALOMA
PURE VEGETABLE SOAP
1 x 125g bar

6
24 finger plasters
Antiseptic pads kill germs
Washproof Plasters

8
PERFECT HANDS
2 NAIL FILES
for natural nails

9

10 white TISSUES
Soft and Fresh

10

Dentacare
DAILY TOOTHPASTE
for sensitive teeth
NEW MINT

12

NUROFEN Tablets
Ibuprofen 200 mg
easy to swallow tablets
fast, effective relief
16 tablets
TARGETED RELIEF FOR PAIN

11

FOR YOUR EYES ONLY
BROWN   long-lasting, easy to use
MASCARA
0.27us fl. oz.   8ml E

2 You see the sign HEALTH CARE as you go into the chemist's. Which of the things in Exercise 1 will you probably find in this department? Which will you find in the TOILETRIES department? Write two lists.

health care: mouthwash,   toiletries: body lotion,

Did you know ...?

chemist's	GB English
drugstore	US English
pharmacy	Australian English
pharmacy	South African English

3 Where will you see these signs? Match them with the two department headings TOILETRIES and HEALTH CARE. Write T or HC in each box.

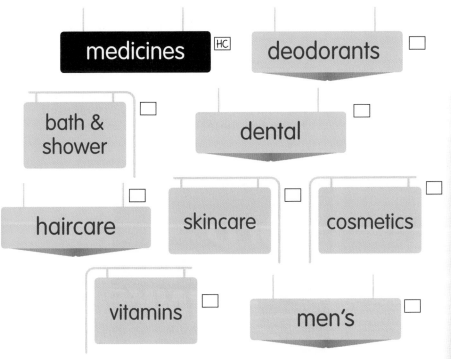

medicines

deodorants

bath & shower

dental

haircare

skincare

cosmetics

vitamins

men's

4 Match the things in Exercise 1 with the signs in Exercise 3. There is more than one thing with some signs and no things with other signs. Write lists.

medicines	plasters, tissues, tablets
deodorants	
bath & shower	
dental	
haircare	
skincare	
cosmetics	
vitamins	
men's	

5 Katka has gone to the chemist's because she needs some of the things in Exercise 1. Look at her bill. Which of the things did she buy?

Katka bought

```
Thank you for shopping at

          Boots

    BAKER STREET  -  774

Served by: MEENA
13/07/2008              12:35

Nurofen Tb 16 G        1.59
R&S shower gel         1.69
Body Ltn Reg 200       2.49

TOTAL TO PAY           5.77
Cash                  10.00
Change                 4.23

┌─────────────────────────────┐
│ You've just missed out on    │
│            24p               │
│ in points to spend in store  │
│                              │
│   Pick up your Instant       │
│     Advantage Card           │
│   today and start saving     │
└─────────────────────────────┘

Boots The Chemists Ltd
   424 4385 0774 133
```

Class bonus

Write a sentence about each of the things in Exercise 1. Begin your sentences with either *You use this/these to …* or *You use this/these if …* . For example: *You use this to wash your hair. / You use this if your hair is dirty.* Exchange your sentences with a partner. Decide which things your friend is describing.

E Xtra practice

Look at the things in your wash bag or in your bathroom. Are the labels in English or in your language? Find the name of the thing in English on the label.

B You'll feel better soon

1 Katka doesn't feel very well. She's got a headache and a cold. She thinks she might be getting flu. What do you think she should do?

I think Katka should ....

Learning tip

We often *skim* a text to find the part of the text which is most useful/important to us. We read the important part slowly, and we probably read some words and sentences more than once in order to understand the details. It is particularly important to read instructions carefully. (See also *Learning tip* in Unit 5.)

2 Katka bought some tablets at the chemist's. Skim the back of the packet and decide if the tablets are suitable for her.

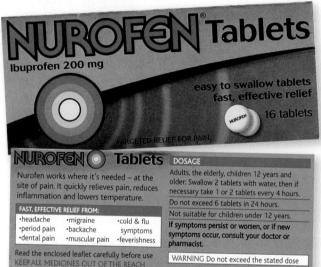

3 Katka wants to know how many tablets she can take and how often. Skim the back of the packet again. Where can she find this information?

....

4 Is this advice correct? Tick ✓ the advice which is correct.

a You should take two tablets the first time. ☑
b You should have a glass of water with the tablets. ☐
c If you don't feel better after 2 hours, you should take 1 or 2 more tablets. ☐
d You mustn't have more than 6 tablets in 24 hours. ☐

Focus on ...
vocabulary

Read what some other people say about their medical problems. Find the name of the problem on the back of the Nurofen packet.

a I get a very bad headache, and sometimes I am sick.
  m i g r a i n e
b I've got a really high temperature.
  _ _ _ _ _ _ _ _ _ _ _
c I think I've pulled a muscle in my leg.
  _ _ _ _ _ _ _ _ _ _ _ _
d I've got toothache. _ _ _ _ _ _ _ _ _ _ _

5 Katka's friend gives her two other products for her cold and headache. Have you ever used things like these? How do you use them?

I've ....
You ....

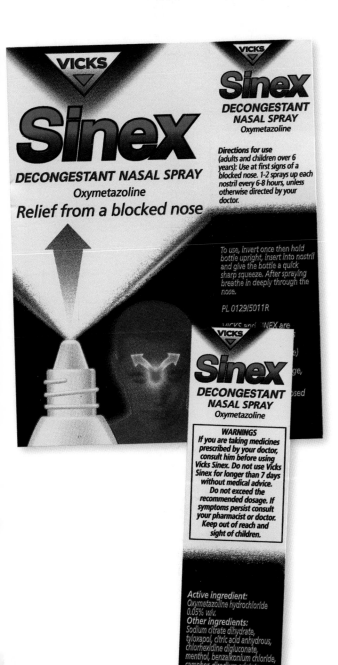

6 Read the backs of the packets and decide if these two products are suitable for someone with a cold and headache.

----

7 Katka wants to know how often to use the nasal spray. Skim the back of the packet again. Where can she find this information?

----

8 Put the pictures into the correct order to show how exactly to use this medication.
1 [c] 2 ☐ 3 ☐ 4 ☐ 5 ☐

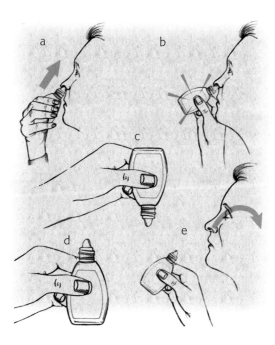

9 Would you use any of these three things – Nurofen tablets®, Cold and flu drink, Vicks nasal spray – if you had a cold, a headache or flu?

Can-do checklist

Tick what you can do.

	Can do	Need more practice
I can identify and find things in a chemist's.	✓	✓
I can skim a text to find the part that is most useful to me.		
I can decide if medication is suitable.		
I can follow instructions on packets.		

Unit 7
Who's it from?

Get ready to read

- When do you usually send a card? Tick ✓ the sentences that are true for you.
  When it is someone's birthday. ☐
  When someone is sick. ☐
  When I want to say 'congratulations'. ☐
  When someone leaves their job or school. ☐
  When I want to say 'good luck'. ☐
  When someone moves to a new house. ☐
  When a member of someone's family dies. ☐
  When I want to say 'thank you'. ☐
  I never send cards. ☐

- When do you usually receive a card? Write your answers.
  When ....
  When ....
  When ....
  When ....

- In which of these ways do you and your friends communicate? Tick ✓ your answers.
  email ☐   letters ☐   notes ☐   postcards ☐
  text messages ☐

go to Useful language p. 84

A I bought this card for you

1 Look at the cards. When would you send each card? Write your answers.

1 When it is someone's birthday.
2 ....
3 ....
4 ....
5 ....
6 ....
7 ....
8 ....

1 Many happy returns of the day!

2 With deepest sympathy

3 Get better soon!

4 New home

5 Good Luck with your exams!

6 sorry you're leaving

7 THANK YOU

8 CONGRATULATIONS

2 Here are the messages inside the cards. Match each message with a card. Write the number in each box.

A ③ B ☐ C ☐ D ☐ E ☐ F ☐ G ☐ H ☐

A

Sorry you're not well, Jaime. We're thinking of you!

Daisuke, Kinga and Sofia

Lucky you! We've got an exam tomorrow!

B

Anna

21 today!!! Have a very happy birthday!

With all my love, Katya

P.S. I won't be at yoga next week, but will see you on the 20th.

C

Dear Oscar

Welcome to your new home! Please knock on our door if you need anything.

All the best,

Luigi and Giovanna

D

Dearest Rosa

I was very sorry to hear that your granddad had died. I am thinking about you a lot at this very sad time.

Love from Eda

E

Rosemary

You are a great teacher! I enjoyed all your classes and I learnt a lot about English grammar. Thanks very much for everything!

Best wishes, Shuang

P.S. You are always welcome in Beijing.

F

Carlos

Hope the new job works out well, and the money is better! The office is quiet without you! Keep in touch!

Adriana and Lola

G

Well done, Alberto! We knew you'd pass!

From all your friends and colleagues at the supermarket!

H

Olav

Hope they're not too awful! Let me know how you got on!

See you at practice on Sunday – don't forget your boots!

Paul

3 Read each message again. Now decide what relationship the sender and the receiver have.

Message A — good friends
Message B — neighbours
Message C — people from the same evening class
Message D — members of the same football team
Message E — students in the same class at college
Message F — work colleagues
Message G — old work colleagues
Message H — student and teacher

4 Who does each sentence describe?

a He's going to take some exams. ___Olav___
b He's just moved house. _____
c One of her relatives has just died. _____
d He's just passed his driving test. _____

5 Write sentences about the other people who received cards.

a Jaime _is ill._____
b Anna _____
c Rosemary _____
d Carlos _____

Focus on ...
pronouns

In message A, there is a pronoun and verb at the beginning of this sentence: *We're thinking of you!* However, there isn't a pronoun and verb at the beginning of this sentence: *Sorry you're not well, Jaime.*

Which pronoun and verb are missing? Tick ✓ the correct box.
I'm ☐ We're ☐ They're ☐ You're ☐ She's ☐ It's ☐

Now read the other messages again. Can you find any more messages with missing pronouns or verbs? What are the missing pronouns or verbs?
Message B (You're) 21 today!
(I) will see you.

Learning tip

When we read a text, we want to understand the writer's message. To do this, we read silently. In real life, we sometimes read aloud – for example, we might read out something interesting from a newspaper to a friend. Reading aloud does not help you to understand the message, but it helps you to practise the language.

6 Now imagine you received all the messages in Exercise 2. Read the messages aloud.

B See you on the 29th!

1 Silvia has received four messages today. Read each message quickly. Complete the sentences with the words in the box.

> an email   a note   a postcard   ~~a text message~~

Message A is _a text message._
Message B is _____
Message C is _____
Message D is _____

A

I'm going tenpin bowling tomorrow night with some friends from work. Do you want to come?
Barbara X

Options   Close

B

🗔 Northern Lights

File   Edit   View   Insert   Format   Tools   Message   Help

To: Silvia Toti
Cc:
Subject: Northern Lights

Hi Silvia

How are you? I've just finished a really fantastic book by a British author called Philip Pullman. You like fantasy, don't you? You'd love this. Do you want to borrow it?

Let me know.

Marcos

C

Silvia

Can you phone your mum? She phoned at 7.30pm. She says it isn't urgent, but she'd like to hear from you. Don't phone after 10pm. She's got a headache, so she's going to bed early.

Margrit

D

Tuesday 23rd June

Hi Silvia

We're having a great time in Scotland. The people are very friendly, but they speak with a strange accent. I can't always understand what they say! We left Edinburgh yesterday and are now heading north. Tomorrow we're going to go looking for the Loch Ness Monster. Have you heard of it?

Say hello to everyone at school. See you on the 29th!

Hans

Ms Silvia Toti
32 King's Road
BRIGHTON
Sussex
BR24 7PQ

Did you know …?

In English we use the title *Mr* for married or single men. We usually say *Mrs* for married women and *Miss* for single women. But some women – married and single – prefer the title *Ms*.

2 Match each message with its function.

Message A — makes an offer.
Message B — makes an invitation.
Message C — describes something.
Message D — makes a request.

3 Tick ✓ the questions that Silvia might ask Barbara.

a Who are you going with? ☐
b Where should I meet you? ☐
c Which day are you going? ☐
d What time are you going? ☐

4 Read message B again. Tick ✓ the sentences that are true for you.

I've heard of Philip Pullman. ☐   I've never heard of Philip Pullman. ☐
I've heard of *Northern Lights*. ☐   I've never heard of *Northern Lights*. ☐
I've already read *Northern Lights*. ☐   I haven't read *Northern Lights*. ☐
I like fantasy. ☐   I don't like fantasy. ☐
I'd love to borrow the book. ☐   I don't want to borrow the book. ☐
                                           I'm too busy to read the book. ☐

5 Imagine you are Silvia. Write a reply to Marcos. Use some of the sentences you ticked in Exercise 4.

Hi Marcos
I'm fine, thanks. How are you? Thanks for your offer. I
_____

6 Circle the correct time in Silvia's note to Margrit.

Margrit. Thanks for your note. I got back at 9.45pm / 10.15pm, so will phone Mum tomorrow. Thanks.
Silvia

7 Read message D. When did Hans and his friends do these things?

a They left Edinburgh on June
_____ .

b They planned to go to Loch Ness on June _____ .

Class bonus

Work with a partner. Act out the conversation between Margrit and Silvia's mum at 7.30pm. Work with a different partner. Act out a conversation between Silvia and Hans on June 29th.

8 Imagine you are Silvia. Which of the four messages would you be most likely to read aloud? Who to? Why?

_____
_____

E✗tra practice

Find out as much as you can about the Loch Ness Monster from the www.nessie.co.uk website. Look at the webpage Recent sightings. What words are used to describe what people saw? Do you really think they saw the monster?

Can-do checklist

Tick what you can do.

	Can do	Need more practice
I can work out the main purposes of cards.		
I can read a message aloud.		
I can understand a message on a card.		
I can identify types of messages.		
I can read a message and respond to it.		

Unit 8
Where can we park?

go to Useful language p. 84

Get ready to read

- Tick ✓ the sentences that are true for you.
  I can drive. ☐
  I've got a car. ☐
  I walk to work/school. ☐
  I've got a bike. ☐
  I use public transport a lot. ☐

- Complete these sentences about travelling into your town/city centre. Use the words in the box.

  | by bike/bus/car/train/underground   on foot |

  The fastest way is ....
  The cheapest way is ....
  The healthiest way is ....
  The best way for the environment is ....

- How do you usually go into the town/city centre? Write your answer.
  ....

A Park & ride

1 **Imagine you are driving from London to Stratford-upon-Avon one Sunday with three friends. You decide to stop in Oxford on the way. How is driving into Oxford made easy? Read the leaflet on the opposite page and tick ✓ the correct description.**

   a You park near the ring road and take a bus into the city centre. ☐
   b You park near the city centre and walk there. ☐

2 **Your friend is giving directions to get to Oxford. Look at the map and put the directions in the correct order. Write the numbers 1–5 in the boxes.**

   a Go past High Wycombe. ☐
   b Take the M40. ☐1

   c There's a car park on the left just before the ring road. ☐

   d Come off at Junction 8. ☐
   e Ignore the turning to Aylesbury. ☐

3 **What is the name of the car park your friend is talking about?**
   ....

4 **Unfortunately the driver does not see the turning to Oxford. Your friend gives him directions. Look at the leaflet and correct your friend's directions.**

   Continue along the M40. Come off at Junction 8. Take the A41 towards Oxford. Turn left at the roundabout. There's a car park on the right. The name of the car park is Pear Tree.

Learning tip

As you read, try to work out the meaning of unknown words. Find other words in the text which might help you with the meaning of the word you do not know. Perhaps some other words in the text have the same meaning – or the opposite meaning. Only use a dictionary to check your guesses.

5 **Here are six words/expressions from the leaflet. Read the leaflet carefully and find the words in the list. Find six other words/expressions which have similar meanings. Sometimes the word in the list comes before the word with a similar meaning; sometimes it comes after.**

   a gateway way to get into
   b most convenient ....
   c frequent ....
   d no charge ....
   e single ....
   f ride ....

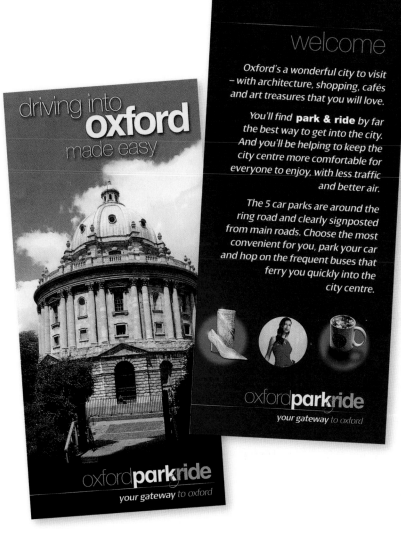

6 Here are two more words/expressions from the leaflet. Find two other words/expressions which have opposite meanings.

a adults ....

b one way ....

7 You arrive at Pear Tree car park and you have to pay. Are your friends' statements true (T) or false (F)? Correct the false statements in your own words.

a We don't have to pay to park. ......

b We can use this 2 to go offer. ......

c Four return tickets will cost £6.40. ......

E X tra practice

Visit the website www.parkandride.net and find out about park and ride in Stratford-upon-Avon. How much does it cost a) to park, b) to ride? How often are the buses?

B Have you got any change?

1 In your country, do you have to pay to park? How do you pay? Tick ✓ one or both of the descriptions below.

a You buy a ticket from a machine and leave your ticket in the car window. ☐
b You take a ticket from a machine and pay when you're ready to leave. ☐

2 Look at the information on the machine below. This is for pay and display parking. Which of the sentences in Exercise 1 describes pay and display?

Did you know ...?

These are British coins. There are 100 pence (p) in a pound (£1). There are also £5, £10, £20 and £50 notes.

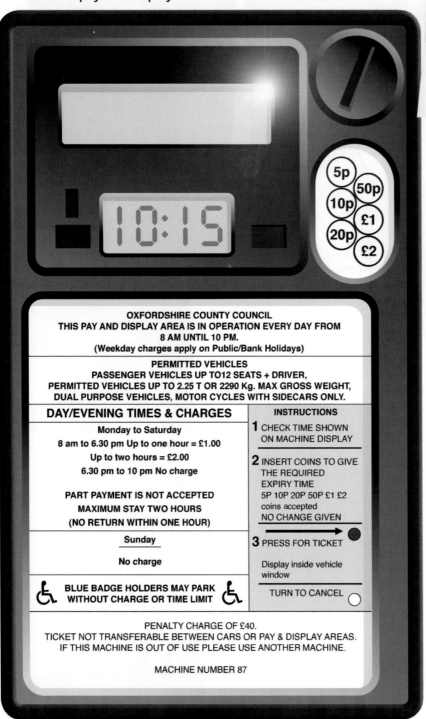

OXFORDSHIRE COUNTY COUNCIL
THIS PAY AND DISPLAY AREA IS IN OPERATION EVERY DAY FROM 8 AM UNTIL 10 PM.
(Weekday charges apply on Public/Bank Holidays)

PERMITTED VEHICLES
PASSENGER VEHICLES UP TO 12 SEATS + DRIVER,
PERMITTED VEHICLES UP TO 2.25 T OR 2290 Kg. MAX GROSS WEIGHT,
DUAL PURPOSE VEHICLES, MOTOR CYCLES WITH SIDECARS ONLY.

DAY/EVENING TIMES & CHARGES	INSTRUCTIONS
Monday to Saturday 8 am to 6.30 pm Up to one hour = £1.00 Up to two hours = £2.00 6.30 pm to 10 pm No charge PART PAYMENT IS NOT ACCEPTED **MAXIMUM STAY TWO HOURS** **(NO RETURN WITHIN ONE HOUR)**	**1** CHECK TIME SHOWN ON MACHINE DISPLAY **2** INSERT COINS TO GIVE THE REQUIRED EXPIRY TIME 5P 10P 20P 50P £1 £2 coins accepted **NO CHANGE GIVEN**
Sunday **No charge**	**3** PRESS FOR TICKET ● Display inside vehicle window
♿ **BLUE BADGE HOLDERS MAY PARK WITHOUT CHARGE OR TIME LIMIT** ♿	TURN TO CANCEL ○

PENALTY CHARGE OF £40.
TICKET NOT TRANSFERABLE BETWEEN CARS OR PAY & DISPLAY AREAS.
IF THIS MACHINE IS OUT OF USE PLEASE USE ANOTHER MACHINE.

MACHINE NUMBER 87

3 It is Wednesday morning and you have decided to go to the Tourist Information Office in the centre of Oxford. You think you will be there for 30 minutes. You are parking in a pay and display area and you are now at the machine. Scan the information on the machine. Circle the answers to the questions.

a What is the minimum amount you can pay?
50p /(£1)/ £2

b You look at the coins in your wallet. You have got one 50p coin, and four 20p coins. How much will you have to put into the machine? Will you get any change?
4 × 20p / 50p + 3 × 20p / all the coins

c If the time on the machine is 10.04 when you pay, when should you return to your car?
10.34 / 11.04 / 12.04

d Should you take your ticket to the Tourist Information Office with you, or should you leave it in your car? Why?
take it / leave it

Focus on ...

no

Find the three expressions with *no* on the pay and display machine. Complete these sentences with the three expressions.

a ....<u>No charge</u>........ means you don't have to pay.

b .... means you mustn't come back.

c .... means you will not get any money back if you insert too much.

Here are some other *no* expressions which you might see when you are travelling around. Match the two halves and make sentences.

d No entry   means you mustn't park here.

e No exit   means you mustn't go down this street.

f No waiting   means you can't get out here.

Class bonus

Look at the photograph. A traffic warden is putting a penalty charge on a car windscreen because the driver doesn't have a valid parking ticket. Imagine this is your car and you arrive as the traffic warden is leaving. What would you say to the traffic warden? How many different excuses can you think of? Make a list and then compare it with other students' lists.

4 You need to park for about two hours. How much will this cost you on these days and at these times? Match the times with the prices.

a Thursday evening, between 6.30pm and 8.30pm   £1

b Friday afternoon, between 2.30pm and 4.30pm   free

c Saturday evening, between 5.45pm and 7.45pm   free

d Sunday morning, between 9.15am and 11.15am   £2

5 How much is a penalty charge for parking incorrectly near a pay and display machine?

....

6 What could happen in these situations? Will you get a penalty charge? Write yes (Y) or no (N). <u>Underline</u> the information on the machine which gives you each answer.

a You have already parked for two hours. You decide to go to the cinema. You put some more money into the machine and take another ticket. ......

b You only want to park for 30 minutes. Someone is leaving and offers you a ticket and you display this ticket inside your car. ......

c The machine near your car isn't working. You decide that you can park for free, and go off to the shops. ......

d You put £2 into the machine and then find that the shop you're going to is closed. You decide to use your ticket in another pay and display area in another part of town. ......

Can-do checklist

Tick what you can do.

	Can do	Need more practice
I can find words with similar meanings in a text.		
I can try and work out the meaning of unknown words.		
I can read a leaflet about parking and work out where to park.		
I can find out about pay and display parking.		

Unit 9
Let's go there

go to Useful language p. 84

Get ready to **read**

- What are the most interesting places to visit in your country? Where can visitors find out about these places?

- The texts in this unit are from Bergen, on the west coast of Norway. They mention Edvard Grieg and fjords. Who was he and what are they? Tick ✓ the box which you think is correct.

  Edvard Grieg was   a   an Arctic explorer. ☐   b   a painter. ☐   c   a composer of music. ☐

  Fjords are   a   mountains near the sea. ☐   b   long narrow pieces of sea between cliffs. ☐
        c   fish that live in the sea around Norway. ☐

A Tourist Information

1 It is Saturday May 10th and you have just arrived in Bergen. The leaflet on the opposite page is in your hotel room. Look at the leaflet quickly and decide what it is about. Tick ✓ the correct box.

  a   what there is to do in Bergen ☐
  b   boat trips up the coast ☐
  c   accommodation in Bergen ☐
  d   Norwegian currency ☐
  e   travel in Norway ☐
  f   the Tourist Information office in Bergen ☐

2 Scan the leaflet again. What does it say about the five other things in Exercise 1? Write sentences.

  a   *You can get all the brochures you will need at Tourist Information.*
  b   ....
  c   ....
  d   ....
  e   ....

3 Scan the leaflet and find the information to complete these sentences.

  a   It's Saturday May 10th. Tourist Information closes at .... this evening.
  b   It opens at .... tomorrow morning.

4 Before you read the leaflet again, think about English grammar. Tick ✓ the sentences you agree with.

  a   Subject pronouns (*I, you, he*, etc.) go before verbs. ✓
  b   Regular plural nouns and third person verbs both end in *s*. ☐
  c   Adjectives go before nouns, and not after them. ☐
  d   The word *the* goes before a noun or an adjective + noun. ☐

5 Find these words in the leaflet. Are they nouns (N) or verbs (V)? How do you know?

building ☒N☒   help ☐   contact ☐   start ☐
offers ☐   display ☐   book ☐   rest ☐

6 One of the words in Exercise 5 ends in the letter *s*. Find all the other words in the leaflet which end in *s*. Decide if the words are verbs or nouns.

treasures (N), ...

7 For each noun in Exercise 6, decide if the word before it is an adjective or another noun. Ignore words which have *the, in, on, and, for* and any verbs before them.

art treasures – art = noun, ...
....

Learning tip

Your knowledge of grammar will not help you with the meaning of unknown words. But it will help you to decide whether words are nouns, verbs, etc. This will help you to link words in sentences and to read words in groups.

---

6   Tourist Information   **B** Bergen Card p. 29

TOURIST INFORMATION

Bergen's Tourist Information office is in the
Fresco Hall opposite the Fish Market.
The building is one of the city's art treasures. We give free help
and advice about what to do in Bergen and all of Norway. We have
all the brochures you will need. Here are some of the things we do:

ARRANGING ACCOMMODATION

In hotels and private houses in Bergen and the surrounding area.

TICKETS FOR TRIPS, CONCERTS AND FJORD TOURS

We are the main contact for trips and harbour excursions in the
city, and we also sell tickets for all the fjord tours departing from
Bergen. In fact, many trips start right outside the door!

Did you know ...?

Norway is one of the few European countries which
is not in the EC (European Community). In 1992,
52% of the population voted against joining.
Switzerland is another non-member.

Focus on ...
uncountable nouns

There are many countable plural nouns in the
leaflet. Find the uncountable nouns *help* and *advice* in
the leaflet. Then find three more uncountable nouns.

Complete these sentences with the uncountable nouns
from the text.

a What's the ____currency____ of Norway? I've only got
  euros.
b Have you got any _____ for less than
  50 kroners per night?
c I'd like some _____ with my luggage.
d I want to buy a guidebook, but I haven't got enough
  _____ .
e Can you give us some _____ about where to
  eat this evening?

Tourist Information   7

THE BERGEN CARD – PRACTICAL AND INEXPENSIVE

Get free offers and/or good discounts with the Bergen
Card. Buy your Bergen Card at the Tourist Information
in Bergen.

Look for **B** on leaflets and notices.

BUY YOUR SOUVENIRS

See the display of Bergen products for sale in the Tourist
Information. We also have a small souvenir shop with a good
selection of traditional souvenirs and gifts. You can also purchase
stamps and telecards.

BUREAU DE CHANGE

You can change your money here. You can also pay for services
with foreign currency.

CAR HIRE

Book a car at the Tourist Information.

TRAIN TICKETS

We sell train tickets for journeys within Norway.

OPENING HOURS 2008		
June, July and August	Daily	08.30–22.00
May and September	Daily	09.00–20.00
Rest of the year Mon–Sat 09.00–16.00		
Closed during Christmas and New Year. *Open during Easter (except Easter Sunday).*		

Information Office also at Bergen Airport all year.

TOURIST INFORMATION IN BERGEN

Vågsallmenning 1, no-5014 Bergen
Tel: (+47) 55 55 20 00 Fax: (+47) 55 55 20 01
E-mail: info@bergen-guide.com – www.bergen-guide.com

**8 Read these sentences from the leaflet silently.
Pause when you reach /. Tick ✓ the best way
to read the sentences.**

a See the display of Bergen / products for sale in the
  Tourist Information. ☐
  See the display / of Bergen products for sale / in the
  Tourist Information. ☐
b We also have a small souvenir / shop with a good
  selection of traditional / souvenirs and gifts. ☐
  We also have a small souvenir shop / with a good
  selection / of traditional souvenirs and gifts. ☐

**9 You have just left your hotel in Bergen. Would
you go to the Tourist Information office?
Why? / Why not? Would you be interested in a
Bergen card?**

E**X**tra practice

Look at www.bergen-guide.com, or choose another city you
would like to go to. Find a place you would like to visit there.

B We've got a choice

1 Here are two leaflets from Bergen Tourist Information. Scan the leaflets.
What can you see in the photos?

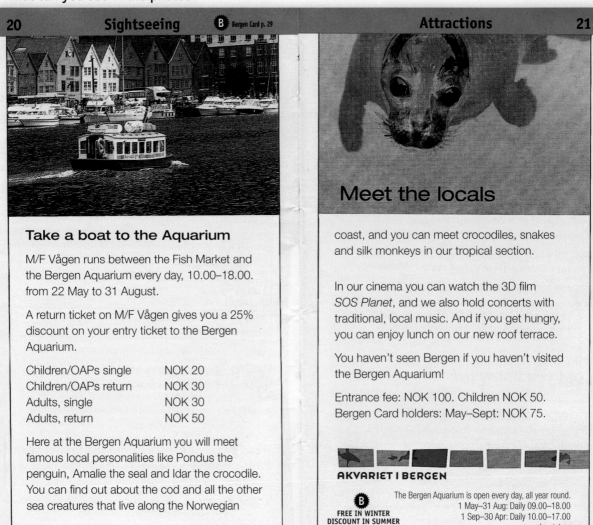

20 · Sightseeing · B Bergen Card p. 29

Take a boat to the Aquarium

M/F Vågen runs between the Fish Market and the Bergen Aquarium every day, 10.00–18.00. from 22 May to 31 August.

A return ticket on M/F Vågen gives you a 25% discount on your entry ticket to the Bergen Aquarium.

Children/OAPs single	NOK 20
Children/OAPs return	NOK 30
Adults, single	NOK 30
Adults, return	NOK 50

Here at the Bergen Aquarium you will meet famous local personalities like Pondus the penguin, Amalie the seal and Idar the crocodile. You can find out about the cod and all the other sea creatures that live along the Norwegian

Attractions · 21

Meet the locals

coast, and you can meet crocodiles, snakes and silk monkeys in our tropical section.

In our cinema you can watch the 3D film *SOS Planet*, and we also hold concerts with traditional, local music. And if you get hungry, you can enjoy lunch on our new roof terrace.

You haven't seen Bergen if you haven't visited the Bergen Aquarium!

Entrance fee: NOK 100. Children NOK 50.
Bergen Card holders: May–Sept: NOK 75.

AKVARIET I BERGEN

B **FREE IN WINTER DISCOUNT IN SUMMER**
The Bergen Aquarium is open every day, all year round.
1 May–31 Aug: Daily 09.00–18.00
1 Sep–30 Apr: Daily 10.00–17.00
www.akvariet.no

2 You are in Bergen on May 12th. Tick ✓ the kinds of transport you can use on May 12th.

a   the boat to the Aquarium ☐
b   the sightseeing coach ☐
c   the cable car ☐

3 You have a Bergen card. Tick ✓ the attraction which gives a discount.

a   the Aquarium ☐
b   the trip to Mount Ulriken ☐

4 Your Bergen card runs out at 12 noon on May 12th. You would like to visit both the Aquarium and Mount Ulriken. Look at the times and prices on the leaflets and decide which attraction you should visit first. Also decide where you would have lunch.

I think I should visit _____

Class bonus

Choose a word from one of the leaflets. Write a dash for each letter of the word, for example
_ _ _ _ _ _ . Your partner says letters from the alphabet, for example *i, o, n, d, s.* If the letter is in the word, write it in the correct place, for example
_ *i n* _ _ _. If the letter isn't in the word, write Ø Ø Ø. How many guesses do you need to work out your partner's word?

| 16 | Sightseeing | Sightseeing | 17 |

The Top of Bergen
Bergen in a Nutshell

All included NOK 150.
(Children half price.)
Cable car only (round trip), NOK 90.

Mount Ulriken (642m) – highest of the 7 mountains

This spectacular round trip takes you from the harbour, through the historic town centre, and up to Bergen's finest panorama. Included in the price:

1 **Bergen Double-Decker sightseeing coach** departs 30m from the Fish Market and the Tourist Information every hour, or more often when needed, from 09.00 to 20.00 in June, July and Aug. In May and Sept. from 09.00 to 17.00.

2 **Bergen Cable Car Ulriken** gives you Bergen's best view! The Cable Car departs every 7 minutes in June, July and Aug. from 09.00 to 21.00, in May and Sept. from 09.00 to 17.00. From Oct. to April from 10.00 to 17.00 on days with good weather.

3 **Mount Ulriken – Mountain concerts: "In the Footsteps of Edvard Grieg".** Ulriken Restaurant & Coffee Bar, indoor and outdoor tables. 5 mini-concerts daily, 15.30–19.30, June–Aug.

Please ask for our special "Bergen in a Nutshell" map & brochure and ticket cards at Tourist Information, hotels, cruise ships, our info table at the bus stop, on the coach and cable car.

Bergen in a Nutshell & Bergen Cable Car Ulriken – Ulriken 1, N–5009 Bergen

Tel +47 5520 2020 Fax +47 5520 2065 – www.ulriken.no – Bergen@ulriken.no

5 Some friends of yours are visiting Bergen in November. Will they be able to visit the Aquarium and Mount Ulriken then? Between what times, and how much will it cost? Complete the chart.

	visit in November	times	price
the Aquarium			
Mount Ulriken			

6 If you could only go to one attraction, which attraction would you prefer to visit? Why?

E**X**tra practice

Find a leaflet in English about a tourist attraction in your town or city. Alternatively, look for something on the Internet. Find out when you can go there and how much it costs.

Can-do checklist

Tick what you can do.

	Can do	Need more practice
I can find out what is available at a Tourist Information office.	✓	✓
I can read a leaflet and find out when the attraction is open and how much it costs.	✓	✓
I can use grammar to help link words in sentences.		

Unit 10
I'd like to register

Get ready to read

- Look at the picture. What is the matter with these people?

- Circle the words so that they are true for you.
  I'm *never / hardly ever / sometimes / often* ill.
  I'm / I'm not registered with a doctor.
  I *never / hardly ever / sometimes / often* see a doctor.

- Look at the picture again.
  Write sentences about yourself.
  I *never / hardly ever / sometimes / often* have …

go to Useful language p. 84 to p. 85

A North Road Medical Centre

1 You see the leaflet on the opposite page on your first visit to a medical centre. Skim the leaflet and decide who it is for? Tick ✓ the correct box.

doctors ☐   nurses ☐   patients ☐   receptionists ☐

2 Some headings are missing from the leaflet. Look at this list of headings and match them with the paragraphs. Skim the text to find the answers. Do not use a dictionary for any unknown vocabulary.

a New Patients ☐ 4   e Home Visits ☐
b Patient Registration ☐   f Appointments ☐
c Opening Times ☐   g Out of Hours Service ☐
d Telephone Advice ☐

3 Imagine you would like to register at this medical centre. Which two paragraphs should you read first? ☐ ☐

4 Read the two paragraphs. Find four things that you should do. Complete these sentences.

a Speak to _____
b Complete a _____ form.
c Complete a medical _____
d Make an _____

Focus on … the passive

Complete these two sentences from the brochure with the passive form.

a Each new patient _____*is asked*_____ to complete a medical questionnaire.
b Most visits by doctors _____ between 12 noon and 3pm.

Rewrite the sentences above in the active form.

c We _____ to complete a medical questionnaire.
d Doctors _____ between 12 noon and 3pm.

Rewrite these sentences in the active form.

e Information about patients is kept on the database.
   We _____
f Minor operations are performed by the doctors at the surgery.
   Doctors _____
g Stop smoking clinics are held twice a year.
   _____
h Health advice is given by nurses and doctors.
   _____

THE MEDICAL CENTRE
Welcome to North Road Medical Centre

1   The medical centre is open from 8.30am until 6pm Monday to Friday. Appointments with the doctors and nurses are available both morning and afternoon.

2   You can make an appointment either in person or by telephone. If you need an appointment urgently, you will be seen on the same day. However, a same-day appointment may not necessarily be with your usual doctor. Patients may be seen by any member of the team.

3   If you would like to register with us, please speak to one of our receptionists. If you decide to register with the medical centre, you will need to complete a registration form. Patients register with the medical centre rather than an individual doctor.

4   Each new patient is asked to complete a medical questionnaire. You should also make an appointment to see one of the nurses for a health check soon after registering. There is sometimes a delay in the transfer of medical records from your previous doctor and this appointment gives us valuable information about your health.

5   The Out of Hours Service is available from 6.30pm until 8am Monday to Friday; at weekends from 6.30pm on Friday to 8am on Monday; and on Bank Holidays. Telephone 0845 345 8995 to contact the Out of Hours Service. They will arrange for a doctor to contact you. Alternatively you can contact NHS Direct (24 hours) on 0845 46 47 for medical advice or via the Internet at www.nhsdirect.nhs.uk

6   You can always get advice over the telephone. Late morning is the best time to contact the doctors and nurses at the medical centre. Alternatively, you may telephone for advice from NHS Direct (24 hours) on 0845 4647.

7   If you are too ill to come to the medical centre, you can arrange a home visit over the telephone. Most visits by doctors are made between 12 noon and 3pm. If you are able to phone before 11am, this helps us to plan the day.

Did you know …?

NHS stands for National Health Service. This began in 1948 and its aim was to provide free medical, dental and hospital services for everyone in Britain. Nowadays not everyone uses the NHS – more and more people have private medical insurance.

Learning tip

When you need to read a difficult text, you will read some words and sentences very carefully. In order to understand difficult parts of texts, it is a good idea to try and put the sentences of the text into your own words.

---

5   **Your friend Giorgio is telling you about the medical centre. Is what he says true (T) or false (F)? Correct the false sentences.**

a   You can have an appointment at the medical centre on Saturdays. _F_
    You can have an appointment on weekdays (Monday to Friday).

b   You can't always see your usual doctor. ......

c   You can only use the Out of Hours Service at weekends. ......

d   You can get medical advice from the NHS website. ......

e   You should phone the medical centre in the afternoon if you want to speak to a doctor or nurse. ......

f   You should try and phone the medical centre before 11am if you need a home visit that day. ......

Class bonus

Write another true sentence about the medical centre to tell your friends. Read your sentences to the class. How many different sentences have you written?

6   **Two weeks after you register, you are unwell. You decide to make an appointment with a doctor. Answer these questions.**

a   How can you make an appointment?
    You

b   Will you be able to see the doctor that day?

c   Which doctor will you be able to see?

7   **What would you do in these situations? What help will you get from the medical centre? Explain in your own words.**

a   You are very ill. You do not think you can get out of bed.

b   You are ill one weekend.

c   You have got a question about some tablets that you found in the bathroom cupboard.

E X tra practice

The leaflet mentions a website www.nhsdirect.nhs.uk. Go to the Mind & body magazine webpage and try one of the interactive tools. Find out how many calories you burn in an hour's aerobics class or find out if you are more than your 'ideal' weight.

B The medical questionnaire

1 You are going to complete a medical questionnaire. This includes the following words. Make sure you know what they mean. Use a dictionary if necessary.

operation pregnancy disability prescription allergy medication heart attack stroke

2 Look at the questionnaire. How many sections are there?

NORTH ROAD MEDICAL CENTRE

ADULT MEDICAL QUESTIONNAIRE

(Please write something in every space.)

The answers to this questionnaire will help us to care for you until your old records arrive.
We like to give all new patients a health check soon after they register.
Please make an appointment at Reception.

PERSONAL INFORMATION
Today's date ....
Surname (last name) .... Title (Mr/Mrs/Miss/Master/Ms) ....
First name ....Marital status ....
Date of birth .... Occupation ....
Address in UK ....
Post code .... Tel. nos. (Home & Work) ....
Name of doctor ....
(with whom you are registering)

1 MEDICAL HISTORY (past and present)
   List (with dates) any serious medical problems. Please include operations, pregnancies and important
   disabilities.
   ....

2 MEDICATION
   Please list any medication you take regularly (whether on prescription or bought over the counter).
   ....

3 ALLERGIES TO MEDICATION
   ....

4 FAMILY HISTORY
   Do heart attacks occur in young members of your family (less than 55 years old)? YES ☐ NO ☐
   Do strokes occur in young members of your family (less than 55 years old)?   YES ☐ NO ☐
   Give details of any illnesses which occur in your family.
   ....

5 SMOKING
   Do you smoke? YES ☐ NO ☐ GIVEN UP ☐
   Daily Amount .... Date Stopped ....

6 ALCOHOL INTAKE (1 unit = ½ pint beer, 1 glass wine or a single measure of spirit)
   How many units do you drink in an average week? 0 ☐ 1–3 ☐ 4–7 ☐ more than 7 ☐

7 What is your WEIGHT? .... HEIGHT? ....

3 Complete the PERSONAL INFORMATION section of the questionnaire for yourself.

4 Complete section 7 for yourself.

5 Read what Giorgio says about himself. Which boxes would he tick in sections 4, 5 and 6?

a My grandfather died of a heart attack when he was 52.

b I don't think anyone in my family has had a stroke.

c I used to smoke 10 cigarettes a day, but I stopped on December 31st 2007.

d I drink a couple of pints during the week, and one or two glasses of wine at the weekend.

6 Giorgio is helping some friends to compete the medical questionnaire. Here is what they want to say. Circle any of the words which are similar to words in your language.

a I have eczema on the back of my hands, especially when I am stressed.
b I don't take any medicines.
c I am allergic to penicillin.
d My grandmother had breast cancer.
e I had appendicitis when I was 14.
f I sometimes take Nurofen® when I have a headache.
g Some people in my family suffer from asthma.
h I am deaf in one ear.
i I take sleeping tablets when I can't sleep.
j Some plasters make my skin very red and itchy.
k My dad has high blood pressure.
l I suffered from depression when my sister died. I couldn't go to work for six months.

7 Match the sentences in Exercise 6 with sections 1–4 of the questionnaire. Write the numbers in the boxes.

a [1]　b [ ]　c [ ]　d [ ]　e [ ]　f [ ]
g [ ]　h [ ]　i [ ]　j [ ]　k [ ]　l [ ]

8 Look at what Giorgio's friends say in Exercise 6. Are any of the sentences true for you? They are probably not completely true, but are some of them similar?

9 Complete the rest of the questionnaire for yourself. If you don't know the words for illnesses, then use the name in your own language – it may be similar to the English word.

Did you know ...?

In Britain, draught beer (beer which comes out of a tap) is sold by the pint. One pint is 0.57 litres. Glasses of wine are measured by the millilitre (from 125ml–375ml).

Can-do checklist

Tick what you can do.

	Can do	Need more practice
I can find out how to register at a medical centre.		
I can find out how to see a doctor.		
I can put the sentences of a text into my own words.		
I can complete a health questionnaire.		

Unit 11
What's on tonight?

Get ready to read

- How much TV do you watch every day? Complete the sentence so that it is true for you.
  I watch .... hour(s) of TV every day.

- Tick ✓ the sentences that are true for you.
  I go to the cinema to see films. ☐
  I watch films on TV. ☐
  I rent DVDs. ☐

- What kind of films do you like? Put these types in order of preference. Write the numbers 1–5 (1 = most like) in the boxes.
  comedy ☐ fantasy ☐ horror ☐ romance ☐
  thrillers ☐

go to Useful language p. 85

A Let's watch this

1 There are lots of different types of programmes on television. (Circle) the programme type in each pair which matches the dictionary definition.

a *game show* /(*documentary*) a film or television programme that gives facts about a real situation or real people
b *chat show* / *soap opera* a television programme about the lives of a group of people that is shown every week
c *drama* / *sitcom* a play on television
d *cartoon* / *quiz show* a game on television in which people answer questions

Learning tip

You can use either a dictionary with English and your language or a dictionary which has definitions in English. The main advantage of using a dictionary which has definitions in English is that you are working in English all the time. These dictionaries also explain the different meanings that one word can have, and they give lots of examples of how words are used.

2 Write each unused programme type from Exercise 1 next to the correct definition.

a .... *sitcom* .... a funny television programme that is about the same group of people every week in different situations
b .... a programme made using characters that are drawn and not real
c .... a programme on television in which people play games or answer questions to try to win prizes
d .... a television programme in which people are asked questions about themselves

3 Which types of programme do you like? Put the eight types of programme in Exercises 1 and 2 into three groups.

I love	I hate	I don't mind

4 Scan the TV guide on the opposite page. Which of the programme types in Exercises 1 and 2 can you find in the guide? (Circle) the words in the guide.

5 What other types of programme are there? Scan the TV guide again. Add these types to the chart in Exercise 3.
news, sports programme

Did you know ...?

There are five main TV channels in Britain. BBC stands for British Broadcasting Corporation and ITV stands for Independent Television. People pay for BBC television by buying a television licence. ITV and Channel 4 get their money from advertising. The fifth channel is called Channel Five and is the newest channel.

BBC1	BBC2	ITV	Channel 4
6.00 BBC News **6.30 Regional News** **7.00 A Question of Sport** David Beckham takes part in tonight's quiz. **7.30 Neighbours** Australian soap opera	**6.00 Animal Park** The zookeepers deal with a lion that likes to climb trees. **7.00 Comedy Doubles Dad's Army / Fawlty Towers** Two more repeats of old sitcoms. Old, but good!	**6.00 London Tonight** **6.30 ITV Evening news** **7.00 Emmerdale** Zak brings together his family to discuss their money problems. First half of an hour of soap. **7.30 Coronation Street** Jason promises Sarah a nice big meal for her birthday.	**6.00 Top Cat** cartoon **6.30 The Simpsons** Lisa enters a singing competition **7.00 Channel 4 News**
8.00 Men Behaving Badly Sitcom starring Martin Clunes **8.30 The Royle Family** More sitcom. A welcome return! **9.00 Poirot** Crime drama with David Suchet. A woman is murdered on a luxury cruise and there is no shortage of suspects.	**8.00 Equator** Simon Reeve concludes his travels with a visit to South America and the Galapagos Islands. **9.00 Genghis Khan** A profile of the Asian conqueror revealing his interest in law and culture.	**8.00 Who Wants To Be A Millionaire?** More contestants try their luck in everyone's favourite game show **9.00 Parkinson** The broadcaster returns with a new series of music and chat. Tonight's special guests include Elton John.	**8.00 Diet Doctors: Inside and Out** Dr Wendy Denning shows how feet reflect a person's health, and proves the dangers of eating too much chocolate. **9.00 Is This the Worst Weather Ever?** Documentary about tornadoes.
10.00 BBC News at Ten **10.30 Regional News and Weather** **10.40 Match of the Day** Portugal v England. Highlights of today's World Cup qualifying matches.	**10.00 Film 2008** Film Review with Jonathan Ross. Reviews of all this week's films. Plus news of Almodóvar's latest release. **10.30 Newsnight** Analysis of today's events. **11.00 FILM: The Perfect Storm** (2000) George Clooney stars as the captain of the Andrea Gail, a fishing boat caught in the worst storm ever.	**10.00 The Complete Guide to Parenting** New comedy series starring Peter Davison. **10.30 ITV News** **11.00 FILM: Spirited Away** (2001) Japanese director Miyazaki's first digitally animated feature. The highest-earning Japanese film ever. Not surprising!	**10.00 CSI: NY** The drama returns. A man's body is found on Brooklyn Bridge. **11.00 The Album Chart Show** Music by Keane.

6 Your flatmate has listed the times and channels he would like to watch this evening. What types of programme does he like?

> 6-7pm Channel 4, 7-8pm BBC2
> 8-9pm BBC1, 10-11pm ITV

My flatmate wants to watch _____
_____

7 Would you like to watch the programmes with him? Why? / Why not?

8 Imagine you are not feeling well and you want to spend the evening at home. (Your flatmate has gone out!) Look at the TV guide and choose what you want to watch. Plan your evening's viewing.

Class bonus

Find out which are the most popular programmes in the TV guide with everyone in your class.

E✗tra practice

Choose some words you don't know from the television guide. Try and work out their meaning. Check your guesses in a dictionary. Try and use a dictionary which has definitions in English.

B Spirited away

1 You see this description of a film in a TV guide. Answer these questions.

a Have you heard of this film?

b Have you seen it?

c Do you know anything about it?

> **11.00 FILM: Spirited Away**
> (2001) Japanese director Miyazaki's first digitally animated feature. The highest-earning Japanese film ever. Not surprising!

2 Look at the dictionary definitions. They may help you to work out what the film is about. What type of film do you think *Spirited Away* is? Tick ✓ one of the boxes. Don't check your answer yet.

a comedy ☐

a romance ☐

a fantasy ☐

> **spirit¹** /'spɪrɪt/ *noun* [NOT ALIVE] [C]
> something which people believe exists but does not have a physical body, such as a ghost *evil spirits*
>
> **spirit²** /'spɪrɪt/ *verb* **be spirited away/out/to, etc**
> to be moved somewhere secretly *He was spirited away to a secret hide-out in Mexico.*

3 Skim the review and check your answer to Exercise 2.

4 Skim the review again. What does the critic think of the film? Tick ✓ the correct box.

a He recommends it. He thinks it's quite good. ☐

b He doesn't recommend it. It's one of the poorest animated films he's seen. ☐

c He recommends it. He thinks it's a fantastic film. ☐

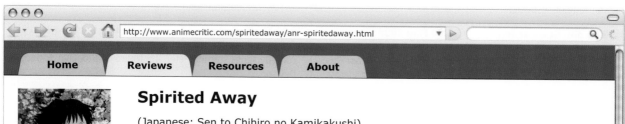

Home   Reviews   Resources   About

http://www.animecritic.com/spiritedaway/anr-spiritedaway.html

Spirited Away

(Japanese: Sen to Chihiro no Kamikakushi)

1 *Spirited Away* begins with Chihiro and her parents travelling to their new home. They take a wrong turn and find themselves in a mysterious town with many restaurants. They can see all kinds of food in the restaurants. Chihiro's parents decide to sit down and they start eating. While they eat and eat, Chihiro explores. She meets a boy named Haku, who tells her to leave the place immediately. But it is too late! Chihiro is trapped in this spirit world and her parents have become animals. She must learn to survive in this strange land and, more importantly, she must try to rescue her parents and return home.

2 The story is about Chihiro's personal growth and the lessons she learns from her experiences in the spirit world. She finds work at a bathhouse run by a stern old woman named Yubaba. As the newest member of the staff, Chihiro is given the hardest jobs. But she responds in a way that we can both admire and believe, and she also makes a few friends at the same time.

3 Everything about this film is gorgeous. The artwork is rich and colourful, and the fantasy world in which Chihiro finds herself is amazing. The animation is lifelike. And, as well as being wonderful to look at, the film has fantastic music by composer Jo Hisaishi.

4 The English voices are great but, with Disney's resources, anything less would be disappointing. The casting is excellent – Daveigh Chase is perfect as Chihiro. There are also memorable performances from Suzanne Pleshette as Yubaba and Susan Egan as Lin.

5 *Spirited Away* is Japan's number 1 film. It has received a number of prizes (including a 2003 Academy Award for "Best Animated Film") – the critics love it. And so do I!

5 Which paragraphs are about the writer's opinion (O)?
Which are about the story (S)?

paragraph 1 [S]　　paragraph 3 [ ]　　paragraph 5 [ ]
paragraph 2 [ ]　　paragraph 4 [ ]

6 What does the critic like about the film? Tick ✓ the boxes.
Make a list of adjectives he uses.

	adjective(s)
a　artwork [ ]	
b　animation [ ]	
c　music [ ]	
d　English voices [ ]	
e　casting [ ]	
f　performances [ ]	

7 Try and work out the meaning of any unknown adjectives in
Exercise 6. Then check your guesses in a dictionary if you
want to.

Focus on …

verb + *to* …

Complete these phrases from the review.
a　Chihiro's parents *decide* _____ to sit _____ down …
b　She must *learn* _____ in this strange land …
c　She must *try* _____ her parents …

Now complete these sentences. Use the past simple form of the verbs in *italics*
above and other suitable verbs.
d　I was thirsty. I _____ a cup of tea.
e　I had lessons and I _____ tennis.
f　I _____ the book, but it was too difficult for me.

---

8 Look at the pictures in
the review. Read the
paragraphs about the story.
Work out the name of the
character in the pictures.

_____

9 Underline the adjectives in
the paragraphs about the
story. Try and work out the
meaning of any unknown
adjectives.

10 Do you think *Spirited
Away* is a good title for the
English-language version of
this film?

_____

11 Who do you think this film
is for? Tick ✓ one of the
boxes. Give reasons for
your answers.

a　It's for children. [ ]
b　It's for adults. [ ]
c　It's for children and adults. [ ]

12 If you haven't already seen
this film, would you like to
see it?

_____

E X tra practice

Look on the Internet for another
review of this film. Does the
reviewer have the same opinion
as this critic? What else do you find
out about the film?

Can-do checklist

Tick what you can do.

	Can do	Need more practice
I can use a dictionary with English definitions.		
I can read a TV guide and choose programmes to watch.		
I can read a film review and understand the writer's opinion.		

A Are these statements true (T) or false (F)?

1 Some English words may mean the same as similar words in your own language. ...... (Unit 1)

2 You do not have to understand every word in a text. ...... (Unit 2)

3 If you want to find a particular piece of information, you will need to read every word of a text in order to find it. ...... (Unit 3)

4 Thinking about the topic of a text in your own language before you start reading can help you understand the text. ...... (Unit 4)

5 If you want to get a general idea of what a text is about, you must read from the beginning and continue to the end. ...... (Unit 5)

6 You must read a text slowly and carefully in order to identify the most important part. ...... (Unit 6)

7 Reading a text aloud always helps you to understand the writer's message. ...... (Unit 7)

8 You can sometimes work out the meaning of unknown words in a text. ...... (Unit 8)

9 Your knowledge of grammar will help you to work out the meaning of an unknown word. ...... (Unit 9)

10 The best way to understand a difficult text is to learn it by heart. ...... (Unit 10)

11 Dictionaries which are only in English contain lots of examples of how to use the language. ...... (Unit 11)

B Now read the *Learning tips* for Units 1–11 on pages 87–89. Do you want to change any of your answers in Exercise A?

C The first time we read a text, we usually either skim or scan it. Can you remember the difference between skimming and scanning? Complete these definitions.

12 If you .... a text, you know exactly what you're looking for. You search through the text quickly until you find that specific piece of information.

13 If you .... a text, you want to get a general idea. You look at the text quickly without focusing on any details.

D Look at this list of real-life reading situations. Circle the text type in each situation. Then decide whether you would skim or scan the text in each situation? Tick ✓ the correct box.

14 Your friend can meet you at Central Railway Station, Sydney at 7pm at the earliest. You're looking at a timetable to find a train which will arrive at a convenient time.
scan ☐ skim ☐

15 Your friend says she'll give you the money for a book you bought her. You're looking at the bill to find the price.
scan ☐ skim ☐

16 You're hungry and you're standing outside a restaurant. You're looking at the menu to decide whether to go in.
scan ☐ skim ☐

17 You're looking at a cinema programme. You want to know if the cinema shows the type of films you like.
scan ☐ skim ☐

18 You're looking at a dictionary. You're trying to decide whether to buy it or not.
scan ☐ skim ☐

19 You've just received a postcard. You want to know who it's from.
scan ☐ skim ☐

E The way we read a text depends on our purpose in reading. Two people can read the same text in a different way. Think about the text types in Exercise D again. Complete the sentences with *scan* or *skim* and the text types.

20 You would .... to find out if your favourite dish is on the menu.

21 You would .... to find out how often the trains are.

22 You would .... to find out what film is showing on Wednesday evening.

23 You would .... to find out the pronunciation of *Mrs*.

24 You would .... to find out if your friends are enjoying their holiday.

25 You would .... to find out if you can throw it away.

F Skim these texts. What is each text, or where does it come from? Choose from the following.

| email   cinema ticket   film review   medical centre leaflet |
| car park ticket   text message   tourist leaflet   TV guide |

26 Text A ------------------------------
27 Text B ------------------------------

G Answer these questions about Text A. Write one, two or three words only.

28 You like quiz shows. Is there one on TV this afternoon?

----

29 It's almost one o'clock. Has a programme just started – or has it just finished?

----

30 How long does the music programme last?

----

31 You think you might watch the film. Who is in it?

----

32 What type of programme is on after the film?

H Are these sentences about Text B true (T) or false (F)?

33 You've bought a new mobile phone.
You should phone the medical centre to give them your new number. ......

34 You've moved within the city, but now live five kilometres from your old house.
You might have to register at another medical centre. ......

35 You need to see a nurse.
Some visits to the nurse need more time than others. ......

36 You need to get some medication.
You can find out about the nearest chemist at the medical centre. ......

37 You'd like to ask a pharmacist about some tablets you're taking.
You must go and speak to the pharmacist during the daytime. ......

Text A

MORE 4

12.50 Countdown Game show
1.30 How Music Works with Howard Goodall World and Fusion Music (R)
2.30 Dinolab Using the latest technology to discover how dinosaurs lived
3.30 Edith Piaf – Singing Her Life Documentary
4.30 FILM Love Happy Stars the Marx Brothers. A group of actors accidentally receive some stolen jewels. A real gem. (1949 B/W)
6.05 Shackleton Stars Kenneth Branagh. Drama recounting the story behind the explorer Ernest Shackleton's 1914 expedition to the South Pole (1/2, R)

Text B

CHANGE OF PERSONAL DETAILS

If you change your name, address or telephone number, please let us know in writing. If you are unsure whether a change of address means you are outside the area for this medical centre, the receptionists can advise you about this.

NURSING SERVICES

The nurses provide a wide range of services during opening hours. Please make an appointment with the receptionist. When booking your appointment with the nurse, it is helpful if you can state your reason for seeing her so that we can book the appropriate amount of time.

LOCAL PHARMACISTS

Your local pharmacist is able to give you free health advice and you don't need to make an appointment. The receptionists will be able to give you details of local chemists. Many pharmacists operate extended hours on a rota basis. Phone NHS Direct on 0845 46 47 for details or look in the local press.

I Skim these texts. What is each text, or where does it come from? Choose from the following.

email	cinema ticket	film review
medical centre leaflet		car park ticket
text message	tourist leaflet	TV guide

38 Text C ....
39 Text D ....
40 Text E ....

Text C

Hello Yolanda

I am home again after my holiday. I am pleased to be back! The weather wasn't great in France, but that wasn't the problem. I broke my leg on the second day of the holiday and couldn't ski after that. I had to stay in the hotel while the others were out all day. I was really bored! When can you come round and see me?

Love Mira

Text D

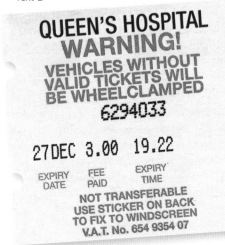

QUEEN'S HOSPITAL
WARNING!
VEHICLES WITHOUT VALID TICKETS WILL BE WHEELCLAMPED
6294033

27 DEC 3.00 19.22

EXPIRY DATE   FEE PAID   EXPIRY TIME

NOT TRANSFERABLE
USE STICKER ON BACK TO FIX TO WINDSCREEN
V.A.T. No. 654 9354 07

Text E

ROTORUA
HERITAGE TOUR
GS40P

HALF-DAY AFTERNOON TOUR
OPERATES DAILY

Experience the scenic beauty of Rotorua's lakes and its volcano. Learn about the history and culture of Rotorua and the devastation caused by the eruption of Mt Tarawera in 1886.

HIGHLIGHTS INCLUDE

- SCENIC BEAUTY Five of Rotorua's lakes, including a view to Mt Tarawera across Lake Tarawera.

- BURIED VILLAGE Enjoy a guided tour of this fascinating location. The Te Wairoa village disappeared when Mt Tarawera erupted. Now you can find out about life in New Zealand of the 1880s.

- ROTORUA MUSEUM Experience a guided tour through the award winning museum. View fascinating exhibits showcasing Rotorua's vibrant volcanic history. Enjoy a short film of the history of Rotorua.

ROTORUA HERITAGE TOUR	TOUR CODE GS40P
ADULT	$89.00
CHILD	$44.50
DEPARTS 12.45pm, Tourism Rotorua, 1167 Fenton Street, Rotorua or refer to back page for your hotel pick-up details	
RETURNS 5.00pm, Tourism Rotorua	
Price includes hotel pick-up and admissions	

J Answer these questions about Text C. Write one, two, three or four words only.

41 Did Mira enjoy her holiday?

----

42 Where did she go?

----

43 What kind of holiday did she go on?

----

44 Did she go on holiday with one friend – or more than one friend?

----

45 Does Yolanda live in the same town as Mira?

K You buy the ticket in Text D at 15.22pm. Read the definition of *valid*. Then decide if the ticket is valid in these situations. Write Y (yes) or N (no).

> **valid** /ˈvælɪd/ *adj*
> A valid ticket or document is legally acceptable: *The ticket is valid for three months.* ⊅Opposite **invalid**

46 if you return to the hospital on 29th December ......

47 if you're in the hospital for about an hour ......

48 if you leave the car in the car park overnight ......

49 if you use it in another car park ......

50 if you give the ticket to someone else when you leave the car park ......

L Answer these questions about Text E. Write one, two or three words only.

51 Can you go on the tour on Sundays?

----

52 How many hours does it last?

----

53 What's the name of the volcano near Rotorua?

----

54 What happened to Te Wairoa in 1886?

----

55 Do you have to pay extra to get into the museum?

M Where would you see these notices? Match the notices with the places. Write the letters in the boxes.

56 medical centre ☐
57 railway station ☐
58 taxi rank ☐
59 sports centre ☐
60 museum ☐
61 street ☐
62 theatre ☐
63 aquarium ☐
64 restaurant ☐
65 ATM ☐

A **DO NOT FEED THE ANIMALS**

B **CITY TAXIS 24 HOUR SERVICE**

C *Wait here to be shown to a table*

D **7.30pm – 9.30pm Adult swimming only**

E **P PRIVATE PARKING ONLY**

F **TONIGHT! SOLD OUT!**

G Sorry This machine is out of use

H *Free admission to all exhibitions for childern*

I **WAIT HERE UNTIL YOUR NAME IS CALLED**

J **Left luggage open 24 hours a day**

N Now match the notices above with the explanations. Write the letters in the boxes.

66 In the evening, children may not come in. ☐
67 You are too late to get a seat for this show. ☐
68 You can leave your suitcase here. ☐
69 You mustn't give the penguins anything to eat. ☐
70 You can get a car at any time. ☐
71 Only adults have to pay here. ☐
72 Patients should take a seat until the doctor is ready. ☐
73 Not all drivers can leave their cars here. ☐
74 You can't get any money here. ☐
75 You mustn't sit down. ☐

O Read the labels and answer the questions.

76 Look at the front of the bottle. What is the name of the product? Choose the correct answer.
   a VIVA SOL ☐
   b SUN CREAM ☐
   c SFB 8 ☐

77 Skim the back of the bottle and find out when you should use this product.
   a before you go into the sun ☐
   b after you've been in the sun ☐
   c when you've got damaged skin ☐

78 Skim the back of the bottle again and find which section tells you how to use the product.
   a Section 1 ☐
   b Section 2 ☐
   c Section 3 ☐

VIVA SOL

❶ **SUN CREAM WITH DEEP PROTECTION SFB**
Stops UVB rays, the principal cause of sunburn. Gives the best protection against UVA rays, which cause premature skin damage.

❷
✓ enhanced UVB/UVA filter system gives the most effective UVA filtration
✓ long-lasting WATER RESISTANT and resists up to 60 minutes in water
✓ easily applied and quickly absorbed
✓ dermatologically approved

❸
VIVA SOL RECOMMENDATIONS
• Find out your protection factor
• Take care not to burn
• Cover up with a hat or T-shirt
• Stay in the shade between 11am and 3pm
• Apply generously before exposure
• Reapply frequently especially after being in the water

This product meets European standards.

P Read the back of the bottle again. Find words or expressions on the back of the bottle which mean the following:

79 most important   ....
80 early   ....
81 the best   ....
82 be careful   ....
83 wear   ....
84 don't go into the sun   ....

Q Read the back of the bottle again. What part of speech are these words? Choose from:

noun   verb   adjective   adverb

85 rays   ....
86 filtration   ....
87 resists   ....
88 apply   ....
89 frequently   ....
90 European   ....

Unit 12
This school sounds good!

Get ready to read

- In which of these countries is English spoken as a first language? Tick ✓ your answers.
  Australia ☐   Canada ☐   New Zealand ☐   United Kingdom ☐   United States of America ☐

- If you decided to do an English course in another country, where would you go?

- What do you know about New Zealand? What is it famous for? Can you name any towns or cities?

go to Useful language p. 85

A Learn English in New Zealand

1 **You are going to look at a website about an organization called Language Schools New Zealand. Scan the homepage and find the answers to these questions.**

a How many schools does Language Schools New Zealand have? _____

b Where are the schools? _____

2 **Scan the homepage again. Answer these questions.**

a Which sections mention the courses? _____

b Which courses does the third section mention?
_____

c Which other course does the other section mention?
_____

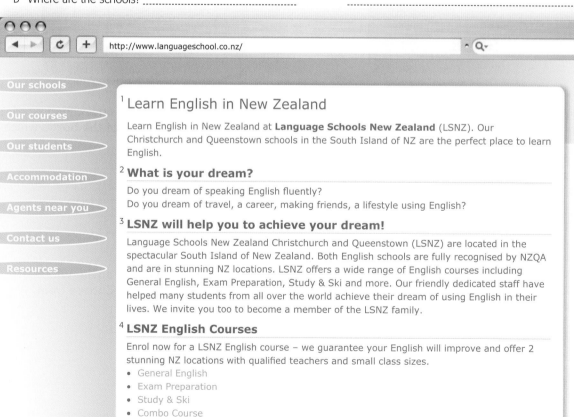

http://www.languageschool.co.nz/

Our schools
Our courses
Our students
Accommodation
Agents near you
Contact us
Resources

¹ Learn English in New Zealand

Learn English in New Zealand at **Language Schools New Zealand** (LSNZ). Our Christchurch and Queenstown schools in the South Island of NZ are the perfect place to learn English.

² **What is your dream?**

Do you dream of speaking English fluently?
Do you dream of travel, a career, making friends, a lifestyle using English?

³ **LSNZ will help you to achieve your dream!**

Language Schools New Zealand Christchurch and Queenstown (LSNZ) are located in the spectacular South Island of New Zealand. Both English schools are fully recognised by NZQA and are in stunning NZ locations. LSNZ offers a wide range of English courses including General English, Exam Preparation, Study & Ski and more. Our friendly dedicated staff have helped many students from all over the world achieve their dream of using English in their lives. We invite you too to become a member of the LSNZ family.

⁴ **LSNZ English Courses**

Enrol now for a LSNZ English course – we guarantee your English will improve and offer 2 stunning NZ locations with qualified teachers and small class sizes.
- General English
- Exam Preparation
- Study & Ski
- Combo Course

IELTS, Cambridge, Toeic & Pitmans Exam preparation courses are offered at both schools.

Learning tip

It is important to try and guess the meaning of words that you do not know. Usually the context (the rest of the text) will help you decide on a possible meaning for them. Don't use a dictionary to find out the meaning of every unknown word, as this takes too long and also interrupts your reading. Only use a dictionary to check your guesses.

3 You decide to read the homepage more carefully. You're not sure about the meaning of some of the words. Find the words on the homepage which have these synonyms (words with similar meaning). Then check the definition of the words you found in a dictionary.

a best (section 1)
   perfect

b easily (section 2)
   ----

c job (section 2)
   ----

d selection (section 3)
   ----

e succeed in (section 3)
   ----

f promise (section 4)
   ----

4 Look at the list of webpages on the homepage. Which webpage would you read next if you wanted to find out more about these things?

a where you can study
   ----

b what you will study
   ----

5 Read the two sections below from the *Our schools* webpage. Complete the sentences with the words *Christchurch* or *Queenstown*. <u>Underline</u> the words on the webpage which give you the answers.

Learn English in Christchurch

Study English right in the heart of Christchurch. Christchurch is New Zealand's 2nd largest city with a population of 345,000. It is well-known for its cultural attractions and is located near beaches. There are many things to do both in the city and in the surrounding areas.

Learn English in Queenstown

Queenstown Language School is situated <u>on the shores of Lake Wakatipu</u>. Queenstown is the adventure capital of the world and is a great place to live and study. It is New Zealand's premier resort, and is world famous for its scenery and its extreme sports. Queenstown is an outdoor paradise. Enjoy magnificent views, fresh air, clean water and a night sky full of stars.

a The LSNZ school in _____Queenstown_____ is very near a lake.
b The LSNZ school is in the middle of _____ .
c More people go on holiday to _____ than any other place in New Zealand.
d There are cinemas, theatres, museums and galleries in _____ .
e _____ is surrounded by mountains, rivers and forests.
f You can do exciting – and sometimes dangerous – sports in
   _____ .
g _____ is near the sea.
h _____ is a healthy place to live and study.

Focus on ...
synonyms

Find these words in the webpages. Some of the words have a similar meaning. Put these words into pairs or groups of three.

~~the perfect place~~   lifestyle   located   spectacular
stunning   dedicated   qualified   well-known
situated   famous   ~~paradise~~ magnificent

the perfect place = paradise

Try and work out the meaning of the other words. Then check your guesses in a dictionary.

6 Would you prefer to study in Queenstown or Christchurch? Why? --

B General English

1 Here are some questions you have about Language Schools New Zealand. What do you think the answers might be?

a Are the courses all full-time, or can you do part-time?
b How many weeks do courses last?
c Can you stay with local families?
d What do you do in the classes?
e How many hours do you study a week?
f How much does it cost?
g Where do most of the students come from?
h Is there a social programme?

Did you know …?

Christchurch and Queenstown are 12 hours ahead of London GMT. Look at these time differences around the world.

Christchurch (New Zealand)	9am Monday
Sydney (Australia)	8am Monday
Vancouver (Canada)	1pm Sunday
New York (USA)	4pm Sunday
London (UK)	9pm Sunday

2 You are going to look at the *General English* webpage in order to find out about this course. Which of the questions in Exercise 1 do you expect this webpage to answer? Tick ✓ the boxes.

a ☐ b ☐ c ☐ d ☐ e ☐ f ☐ g ☐ h ☐

3 Look at the *General English* webpage. The answers to some – but not all – of the questions in Exercise 1 are on this webpage. Find the answers.

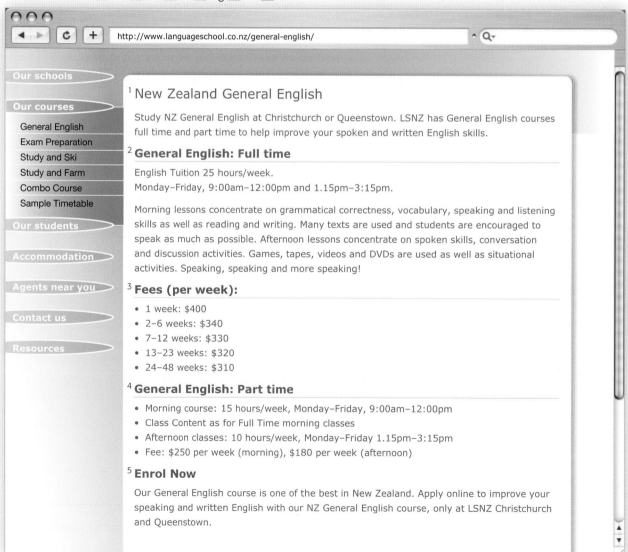

http://www.languageschool.co.nz/general-english/

Our schools
Our courses
  General English
  Exam Preparation
  Study and Ski
  Study and Farm
  Combo Course
  Sample Timetable
Our students
Accommodation
Agents near you
Contact us
Resources

[1] **New Zealand General English**

Study NZ General English at Christchurch or Queenstown. LSNZ has General English courses full time and part time to help improve your spoken and written English skills.

[2] **General English: Full time**

English Tuition 25 hours/week.
Monday–Friday, 9:00am–12:00pm and 1.15pm–3:15pm.

Morning lessons concentrate on grammatical correctness, vocabulary, speaking and listening skills as well as reading and writing. Many texts are used and students are encouraged to speak as much as possible. Afternoon lessons concentrate on spoken skills, conversation and discussion activities. Games, tapes, videos and DVDs are used as well as situational activities. Speaking, speaking and more speaking!

[3] **Fees (per week):**

- 1 week: $400
- 2–6 weeks: $340
- 7–12 weeks: $330
- 13–23 weeks: $320
- 24–48 weeks: $310

[4] **General English: Part time**

- Morning course: 15 hours/week, Monday–Friday, 9:00am–12:00pm
- Class Content as for Full Time morning classes
- Afternoon classes: 10 hours/week, Monday–Friday 1.15pm–3:15pm
- Fee: $250 per week (morning), $180 per week (afternoon)

[5] **Enrol Now**

Our General English course is one of the best in New Zealand. Apply online to improve your speaking and written English with our NZ General English course, only at LSNZ Christchurch and Queenstown.

4 Choose courses for these friends of yours, Omar, Ji-Koo and Hana. Look at the notes about the courses they would like to take. Complete the chart.

	course	cost per week	hours per week
Omar	4 weeks, part-time, focus on grammar and vocabulary	$250	
Ji-Koo	full-time, two weeks	$680	
Hana	10 weeks, afternoons only		

Class bonus

Choose a course for yourself and make notes. Exchange your notes with another student. Work out how much your friend will pay and how many hours they will study.

5 You decide to find out more about the school in Queenstown. Read part of the webpage. Does it answer any more of the questions in Exercise 1?

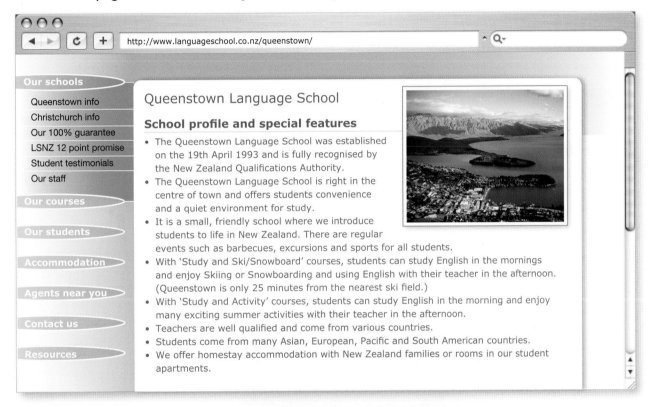

Queenstown Language School

School profile and special features

- The Queenstown Language School was established on the 19th April 1993 and is fully recognised by the New Zealand Qualifications Authority.
- The Queenstown Language School is right in the centre of town and offers students convenience and a quiet environment for study.
- It is a small, friendly school where we introduce students to life in New Zealand. There are regular events such as barbecues, excursions and sports for all students.
- With 'Study and Ski/Snowboard' courses, students can study English in the mornings and enjoy Skiing or Snowboarding and using English with their teacher in the afternoon. (Queenstown is only 25 minutes from the nearest ski field.)
- With 'Study and Activity' courses, students can study English in the morning and enjoy many exciting summer activities with their teacher in the afternoon.
- Teachers are well qualified and come from various countries.
- Students come from many Asian, European, Pacific and South American countries.
- We offer homestay accommodation with New Zealand families or rooms in our student apartments.

Sidebar: Our schools — Queenstown info — Christchurch info — Our 100% guarantee — LSNZ 12 point promise — Student testimonials — Our staff — Our courses — Our students — Accommodation — Agents near you — Contact us — Resources

URL: http://www.languageschool.co.nz/queenstown/

E✗tra practice

Look at the Language Schools New Zealand website www.languageschool.co.nz. Read about homestay accommodation and apartments. Where would you prefer to live?

Can-do checklist

Tick what you can do.

	Can do	Need more practice
I can find out about a language school from its website.	✔	✔
I can guess the meaning of new words from the context.		
I can choose a language course.		

Unit 13
I've chosen this one!

Get ready to read

- Are you reading a book at the moment? What is its title?

- Which of these types of book would you choose to read? Tick ✓ your answers.
  a murder mystery ☐   a thriller ☐   science fiction ☐   romance ☐

- Have you ever read a book in English? What was its title? What type of book was it?

----

go to Useful language p. 85

A Choosing a reader

1 **Look at the four book covers. These are graded readers at just the right level for you. Match the covers with the types of book. Do not check your answers yet.**

   1 A Picture to Remember ———— murder mystery
   2 Hotel Casanova ———————— thriller
   3 Inspector Logan   science fiction
   4 Superbird   romance

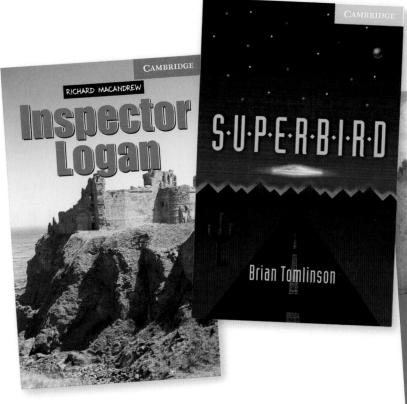

2 Here are some words from the four books. Match each word with the book you think it is in. Which of the words are for something you can see on the cover (C)? Do not check your answers yet.

~~astronaut~~   ~~body~~   ~~castle~~   ~~desert~~   exhibition   flower
gondolas   love   museum   painting   planet   police
reception   sea   spaceship   Venice

1 A Picture to Remember ⎯⎯⎯⎯⎯⎯⎯⎯⎯⎯⎯⎯⎯⎯
2 Hotel Casanova ⎯⎯⎯⎯⎯⎯⎯⎯⎯⎯⎯⎯⎯⎯⎯⎯⎯
3 Inspector Logan body, castle (C), ⎯⎯⎯⎯⎯⎯⎯⎯
4 Superbird astronaut, desert (C), ⎯⎯⎯⎯⎯⎯⎯⎯

Class bonus

Choose a word from Exercise 2. Your partner must ask you questions to find out the word you have chosen. Answers can only be *yes* or *no*. For example: *Is it a place? (yes) Is it a place in a hotel? (no) Do you find old things there? (yes) Is it the … ? (yes)*

3 Read the back cover blurb of the four books. Match the blurbs with the book titles. Do not check your answers yet.

1 A Picture to Remember ☐
2 Hotel Casanova ☐
3 Inspector Logan ☐
4 Superbird ☐

C

CAMBRIDGE English Readers — Beginner/Elementary

'When did your wife go out?' asked Jenny Logan. She looked at the man across the table from her. 'Yesterday,' he replied. 'And she didn't come home last night?' said Logan. 'That's right,' said the man.

It was Jenny Logan's first day in her new job. She was an inspector in the Edinburgh police. It was also her first murder.

A

CAMBRIDGE English Readers — Beginner/Elementary

Dino was 21 and worked in a hotel in the beautiful city of Venice. The women who came to the hotel liked to talk to him. Dino was kind to them. But he knew what he wanted. 'When I'm 26,' he thought, 'I'm going to meet a woman, the woman I want to marry.' Then Dino met Carla and . . .

D

CAMBRIDGE English Readers — Elementary/Lower-intermediate

Cristina Rinaldi works for the Museo Nacional de Bellas Artes in Buenos Aires. She loves art and is happy with her life. Then one day she has a motorbike accident and can't remember some things. But there are two men who think she remembers too much, and they want to kill her before she tells the police what she saw.

B

CAMBRIDGE English Readers — Elementary/Lower-intermediate

A spaceship crashes on a strange planet and everyone on it dies – except for one person. She helps the people of the planet to build their own spaceship, and returns home in it. But when she is back home with her own people, the real trouble begins.

4 Now that you have read the back cover blurbs, look at your answers to Exercises 1 and 2 again. Do the blurbs help you check your answers?

5 Which book would you most like to read?

Did you know …?

The painting on the front cover of *A Picture to Remember* is called *Poppy Field*. It was painted by the Impressionist painter Claude Monet in 1873. The red flowers are poppies.

B A Picture to Remember

1 You are going to read part of the first chapter of *A Picture to Remember*. What do you already know about this story? Look back at pages 64–65 if necessary.

2 Read the first part of the story on the opposite page. Start at the beginning and continue to the end without stopping.

3 The sentences below in *italics* are in the story. Read the sentences and answer the questions.

a *The director of the museum asked Cristina to come into his office.* Why?
He wanted to talk to her about an important job.

b *Cristina couldn't wait to begin.* To begin what?

c *After work Cristina got onto her motorbike outside the museum.* Where was she going?

d *She hoped her father would never see her without it.* Without what?

e Cristina stopped at some traffic lights. *She couldn't believe her eyes.* Why not? What could she see?

f *She looked into his eyes*, and what did he do?

g What did she see on his neck?

h *Cristina felt afraid.* Why?

i *Suddenly a taxi hit the back of her bike.* How did this happen? What happened next?

4 What do you think will happen next?

Learning tip

Extensive reading – reading stories – should be a pleasure! Do not choose a reader with too many difficult words and structures. Read part of the first chapter before you buy or borrow a book – and find out if it's the right level for you. Try to read whole sections – pages, chapters, etc. – without stopping. Aim to get a general overall understanding of the story. When you have done this, you can go back and read the text again more slowly and carefully if you need to.

Focus on ...
irregular verbs

Find the irregular past simple form of these verbs in the story.

a speak ......spoke......   d get ....
b say ....   e have ....
c feel ....

Find five more irregular past simple forms in the story. Write the infinitive form.

f r _ _ _ ....   i f _ _ _ _ _ ....
g w _ _ _ ....   j b _ _ _ _ ....
h g _ _ _ ....

Find five more irregular past simple forms in the story. Write the infinitive form.

k _ _ _ ....   n _ _ _ _ ....
l _ _ _ _ _ ....   o _ _ _ _ ....
m _ _ _ ....

Complete these sentences with five of the verbs.

p When it was my teacher's birthday, I .... her a card.
q Two days ago I .... to my parents on the phone.
r I .... very tired when I work up this morning.
s On my way home last night, I .... a very bright star in the sky.
t I've got a new jacket and I .... it when I went out yesterday.

Extra practice

You can find the rest of this chapter and chapters from lots of other readers on the Cambridge English Readers website www.cambridge.org/elt/readers/worksheets_lesson_plans.asp. You will also find worksheets and a placement test which will tell you your level.

Chapter 1 *Cristina's motorbike*

At eleven o'clock one morning the director of the Museo Nacional de Bellas Artes in Buenos Aires, Leonardo Martinez, asked Cristina Rinaldi to come into his office.

'I want to talk to you about an important job I'd like you to do, Cristina. I think you'll be interested in it.'

'Of course. What is it?'

'A museum in Paris wants to send some Impressionist paintings to Buenos Aires. I spoke to the Paris museum director, Philippe Maudet, this morning and he's interested in using our museum to show the paintings. It's an important job. Would you like to do it?'

'Of course I would. Great! You know I'd love to see Impressionist paintings here in the museum,' answered Cristina.

'Good. I want you to begin work as soon as you can,' the director said. 'There is a lot you'll need to do.'

Cristina felt good all day. She loved Impressionist paintings. This new exhibition was wonderful. She couldn't wait to begin.

After work Cristina got onto her motorbike outside the museum. She was feeling good. She had an important new job, the sun was warm on her back and it was the start of spring weather in the city of Buenos Aires. Maybe tomorrow she could leave her jacket at home. This year September was warm, and people were already talking about a hot summer. Cristina started her motorbike and felt the warm air on her face as she rode along Avenida del Libertador. She never wore a helmet because she liked the feeling of the wind in her long hair. But her father didn't know that. She remembered his words when he gave her the new motorbike: 'Always wear your helmet, Cristina – every time you ride!' She hoped her father would never see her without it.

Every day at this time Cristina rode down Avenida del Libertador to the gym at the Recoleta Health Club. Her day's work at the museum was finished and she was free. She usually forgot about her work as she rode down the Avenida. But today was a little different. She couldn't stop thinking about her new job.

Cristina began to slow down for the traffic lights. The traffic in the city centre was terrible. She didn't work far from the gym but the road had so many traffic lights. She stopped and looked into the car next to her. She saw two men in the car. She couldn't believe her eyes. One of the men had a gun. Then he looked out of the window at Cristina. She looked into his eyes, into his dark brown eyes and for a moment the man looked back. Then he turned his head and she saw a tattoo of a flower, a red poppy, on his neck.

Then she heard the sound of police cars. The man in the car lifted up his gun. Cristina felt afraid. She wanted to go quickly. She tried to start her bike but she couldn't. Everybody else was moving but she couldn't. Suddenly a taxi hit the back of her bike. She fell from the bike onto the front of the taxi and then down onto the road. Her head hit the road hard. She saw nothing, she felt nothing – she didn't even hear the sound of the ambulance which took her to hospital.

Can-do checklist

Tick what you can do.

	Can do	Need more practice
I can use the cover and blurb of a book to predict its type and topic.	✓	✓
I can choose a reader.		
I can read whole sections of a story without stopping.	✓	✓

Unit 14
Use a pencil!

Get ready to read

- Choose the options which are true for you.
  I have been a student of English for *less than one year / one year / two years / more than two years*.
  I have taken / I have never taken an English exam.

- As a student of English, what are you good at and what are you not good at? Rate these skills from 1 (what you are best at) to 6 (what you are worst at).
  reading ☐ writing ☐ listening ☐ speaking ☐
  grammar ☐ vocabulary ☐

go to Useful language p. 85

A Is this exam for me?

1 Your English teacher tells you that there is an English exam you could take. It is suitable for students of your level. Write three questions that you want to ask your teacher about the exam itself. Begin with *How many, When, Which,* etc.

----

2 Look at these questions. Are your questions the same – or similar?

a How many papers are there in the exam?
b Which paper takes the most time?
c Which paper has the most marks?

3 Read the general description of the Key English Test (KET) exam on the right quickly. Answer the questions in Exercise 2.

4 Read below what six students have said about the KET exam. Then read the description of the exam again more carefully and decide if what the people say is true (T) or false (F). <u>Underline</u> the information in the description that gives you the answer.

a A Pass with Merit is better than a Pass. ......
b Not everyone passes the KET exam. ......
c If you fail the exam, you will be told where you are weak. ......
d There are more parts for reading than writing. ......
e You have to listen to a cassette or CD in the listening paper. ......
f You do the speaking test with another student. ......

Content of the KET examination

The KET examination consists of three papers – Paper 1 Reading and Writing, Paper 2 Listening and Paper 3 Speaking.

There are four grades: Pass with Merit (about 85% of the total marks); Pass (about 70% of the total marks); Narrow Fail (about 5% below the pass mark); Fail. For a Pass with Merit and Pass, the results slip shows the papers in which you did particularly well; for a Narrow Fail and Fail, the results slip shows the papers in which you were weak.

Paper 1 Reading and Writing 1 hour 10 minutes
(50% of the total marks)

There are nine parts in this paper and they are always in the same order. Parts 1–5 test a range of reading skills and Parts 6–9 test basic writing skills. You write all your answers on the answer sheet.

Paper 2 Listening about 30 minutes, including 8 minutes to transfer answers
(25% of the total marks)

There are five parts in this paper and they are always in the same order. You hear each recording twice. You write your answers on the answer sheet at the end of the test.

Paper 3 Speaking 8–10 minutes for a pair of students
(25% of the total marks)

There are two parts to the test and they are always in the same order. There are two candidates and two examiners. Only one of the examiners asks the questions.

6 CONTENT OF THE KET EXAMINATION

5 Read the description of one paper below. Which paper is this?

Part	Task Type	Number of Questions	Task Format
Reading Part 1	Matching	5	You match five sentences to eight notices.
Reading Part 2	Multiple choice (A, B or C)	5	You choose the right words to complete five sentences.
Reading Part 3	Multiple choice (A, B or C) AND	5	You choose the right answer to complete short conversational exchanges.
	Matching	5	You choose five answers from eight to complete a conversation.
Reading Part 4	Right / Wrong / Doesn't say OR Multiple choice (A, B or C)	7	You answer seven questions on a text that is up to 230 words long.
Reading Part 5	Multiple choice (A, B or C)	8	You choose the right words to complete eight spaces in a short text.
Writing Part 6	Word completion	5	You decide which words go with five definitions and spell them correctly.
Writing Part 7	Open cloze	10	You fill ten spaces in a text such as a postcard with single words, spelled correctly.
Writing Part 8	Information transfer	5	You complete a set of notes or a form with information from one or two texts.
Writing Part 9	Short message (5 marks)	1	You write a short message, such as a note or postcard (25–35 words), which includes three pieces of information.

Focus on ...
prepositions

(Circle) the preposition in these sentences from the text on the left.
a You match five sentences in / on / to eight notices.
b You choose five answers from / of / with eight to complete a conversation.
Find the other prepositions in the text.

Complete these sentences with prepositions.
c You answer five questions .... a conversation between two speakers.
d You match five questions .... eight possible answers.
e You complete five spaces .... two sets .... notes. There are two speakers.

6 Look at parts of some exam tasks below. Match the tasks with the parts of the exam in Exercise 5.

A ......Part 4......
B ....
C ....

A

Read the article about the Edinburgh Festival. Are the sentences 'Right' (A) or 'Wrong' (B)? If there is not enough information to answer 'Right' (A) or 'Wrong' (B), choose 'Doesn't say' (C).

Visit the Edinburgh Festival!

Every year thousands of people come to Edinburgh, the capital city of Scotland, to be part of the Edinburgh Festival. For three weeks every August and September the city is filled with actors and artists from all over the world. They come to Edinburgh for the biggest arts festival in Britain. During this time the streets of the city are alive with music and dance.

1 The Edinburgh Festival is a month long.

  A Right   **B** Wrong   **C** Doesn't say

2 The Edinburgh Festival is in October.

  A Right   **B** Wrong   **C** Doesn't say

B

Read the sentences about going to a restaurant. Choose the best word (A, B or C) for each space.

1 A new restaurant has just .... near our house.
  A come   **B** begun   **C** opened

2 One day, we decided to go there for a ....
  A plate   **B** meal   **C** dish

C

Complete the conversations. Choose A, B or C.

1 Congratulations!
  A I'm sorry.
  B Thank you.
  C What a pity!

2 I'd like to try those shoes on, please.
  A What size are you?
  B Are they black?
  C Do you like it?

7 Do the exam tasks on these pages.

Class bonus

Write an extra item for the exam tasks A–C. Exchange your items with a partner. Do your partner's items. Then check your answers together.

B Is it A, B or C?

1 Look at these two sections of a KET Reading and Writing paper. Answer these questions.

  a Which section do you read only? _____

  b Which section do you write on? _____

Learning tip

Make sure you read exam instructions very carefully. As well as telling you what to do, exam instructions sometimes give you important information about the topic. Always look at examples. They show you what to do. In matching tasks, they also show which answer cannot be used again.

Section 1

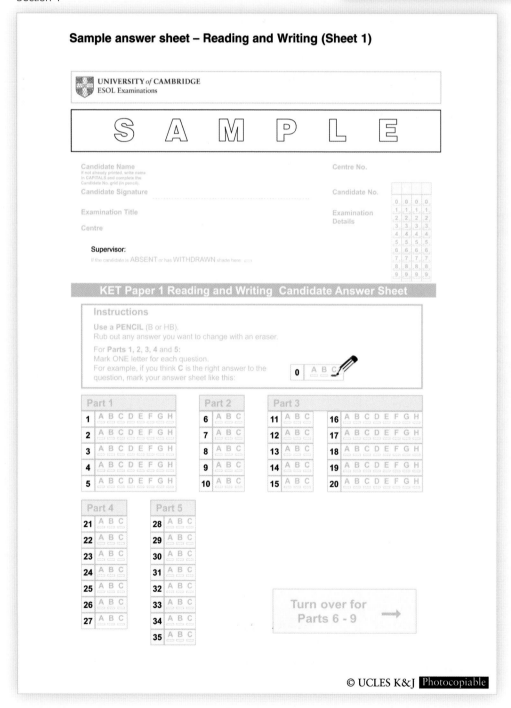

Section 2

Test 1

PAPER 1 READING AND WRITING (1 hour 10 minutes)

PART 1

QUESTIONS 1–5

Which notice (A–H) says this (1–5)?
For questions 1–5, mark the correct letter A–H on the answer sheet.

EXAMPLE	ANSWER
0 We can answer your questions.	E

1   You can't drive this way.

2   Children do not have to pay.

3   You can shop here six days a week.

4   Be careful when you stand up.

5   We work quickly.

A   **Adults £2.50**
    Under 12s FREE

B   Shoes repaired while you wait

C   MIND YOUR HEAD

D   Open 24 hours a day

E   INFORMATION

F   **Police Notice**
    Road Closed

G   **Open daily 10–6**
    (except Mondays)

H   WAITING ROOM

PART 5

QUESTIONS 28–35

Read the information about Madame Tussaud's museum in London.
Choose the best word (A, B or C) for each space (28–35).
For questions 28–35, mark A, B or C on the answer sheet.

Madame Tussaud's

One very famous place for tourists in London is Madame Tussaud's museum. Here people __0__ see figures of famous people made of wax.

Madame Tussaud was born __28__ France in 1761. Her uncle, a doctor, __29__ wax figures of people. He opened __30__ museum of these figures in Paris. Marie helped __31__ in his work.

In 1789, during the French Revolution, Marie __32__ sent to prison. Here she had to copy __33__ heads of famous people when they were dead, including Queen Marie Antoinette's.

In 1795, Marie married François Tussaud __34__ in 1802 she came to London with her wax figures. Here she opened a museum and her figures can __35__ be seen today.

EXAMPLE   ANSWER

0	A	can	B	must	C	shall	A

28	A	at	B	by	C	in
29	A	make	B	made	C	makes
30	A	a	B	one	C	some
31	A	her	B	him	C	them
32	A	has	B	is	C	was
33	A	any	B	the	C	those
34	A	and	B	because	C	when
35	A	ever	B	still	C	yet

2 Read the instructions carefully and do the exam tasks above.

E✗tra practice

You can find out more information about the KET exam on the Cambridge ESOL website www.cambridgeesol.org/exams.

Did you know …?

About 30,000 candidates take the KET exam every year. These people come from more than 60 countries. About 75% of KET candidates are 18 or under. A further 20% are in the 19–30 age group. Approximately 60% are female.

Can-do checklist

Tick what you can do.

	Can do	Need more practice
I can read and understand a description of the KET exam.	✓	✓
I can identify exam tasks.		
I can follow exam instructions and do the tasks.		

Unit 15
It's on the noticeboard

Get ready to read

- Which of these notices would you find on a school noticeboard (S)? Which would you find on an office noticeboard (O)? Which might you find on both (B)?

  a class lists ..S..
  b flats/rooms to rent ......
  c holiday dates and arrangements ......
  d items for sale or wanted ......
  e list of visitors ......
  f new members of staff ......
  g protecting the environment ......
  h services offered (translation, plumbing, etc.) ......
  i student card benefits ......
  j trips ......

- Look at these things you might see in an office. Match the words with the pictures. Write the letters in the boxes.

  1 computer [e]   2 desk-light ☐   3 drink can ☐   4 envelopes ☐
  5 fax machine ☐   6 heater ☐   7 paper clips ☐   8 cartridges ☐
  9 mug ☐   10 newspaper ☐   11 rubber bands ☐   12 plastic wallets ☐
  13 post-it notes ☐ 14 printer ☐

go to Useful language p. 86

A Contact Sobia Iqbal

1 **Look at the notice from an office noticeboard on the opposite page. Which topic in *Get ready to read* is it about?**

----

2 **What is the difference between saving paper and recycling paper? Complete these sentences in your own words. Use the dictionary definitions to help you if necessary.**

If you save paper, you …
If you recycle paper, you …

> **recycle** /ˌriːˈsaɪkl/ *verb* (*present participle* **recycling**, *past* **recycled**) to use paper, glass, plastic, etc again and not throw it away: *We recycle all our newspapers and bottles.*

> **save** /seɪv/ *verb* (*present participle* **saving**, *past* **saved**) **save money/space/time, etc** to reduce the amount of money/space/time, etc that you have to use: *You'll save time by doing it yourself.*

3 **Read Section A of the notice. Which tips are about saving paper (S)? Which tips are about recycling paper (R)? Write the letters.**

   1 ...... 2 ...... 3 ...... 4 ...... 5 ...... 6 ...... 7 ......
   8 ...... 9 ......

4 **Which tips in Section A are for users of computers? Tick ✓ your answers.**

   1☐ 2☐ 3☐ 4☐ 5☐ 6☐ 7☐ 8☐ 9☐

5 **Read Section B. Which of the office items in *Get ready to read* are mentioned here?**

   paper clips, --

Environmental tips for the workplace

If you have any other tips about how to save resources in the workplace, please contact Sobia Iqbal (Office Services Manager) on extension 2043. This notice will be revised later this year.

A Saving and recycling paper

1. Use scrap paper for notes instead of Post-it notes where possible. If you need Post-its, try the small ones.
2. Try not to print out every email; read it on screen instead.
3. Check the length of your email before printing it – cut and paste it into Word.
4. Print documents on both sides (where possible).
5. Re-use scrap paper in the fax machine.
6. Email minutes and reports rather than send round paper copies.
7. Send documents electronically rather than by post.
8. Put newspapers, notes and other paper items into the recycling bin.
9. Don't put envelopes into the recycling bin.

B General recycling

1. Re-use paper clips, plastic wallets, rubber bands, etc.
2. Recycle cartridges from the printer – simply return them to Office Services.
3. Use internal mail envelopes wherever possible. Use each one as many times as possible.
4. Always use the recycling bin for your aluminium drink cans from the machine.
5. Use your own mug in order to reduce the number of plastic cups needed.

C Saving energy

1. Use heaters and desk-lights only when they are needed.
2. Turn off computers before leaving for the weekend.
3. Switch off lights and heaters when not in use.

Focus on ...
nouns and verbs

Read the notice again. How many times:
can you find the word *use*? _____ is it a noun? _____

Find these words in the notice. Are they nouns (N) or verbs (V)?
contact __V__ need _____ check _____ cut _____ paste _____ print _____ post _____

Complete the sentences with the seven words above. Is each word a noun (N) or a verb (V)? Write the letters on the lines.
a There's no _____need_____ to phone Jim. I've already spoken to him. __N__
b Susan James is my main _____ at Smiths. She's the person I phone. _____
c I'll buy some stamps, then I'll _____ these letters. _____
d That's a nasty _____ you've got on your hand. _____
e We do a _____ on the fire alarm every week. _____
f The _____ in this book is a nice size. I can read it quite easily. _____
g You can't recycle envelopes because of the _____ on them. _____

Which other word in the notice is both a noun and a verb? _____

---

6. **Write a sentence about saving or recycling each item in Exercise 5. Use *save* or *recycle* in each sentence.**

   Recycle paper clips, plastic _____
   wallets and rubber bands. _____

   ----

7. **What should employees do if they have another tip for the notice? Complete the sentence.**

   If you have another tip for the _____
   notice, _____
   ----

8. **Here are three more tips for the notice. Which sections should they go in – A, B or C?**

   a Use noticeboards rather than circulating non-urgent memos. ......
   b Photocopy instead of printing out lots of copies. ......
   c Position desks and workstations near windows to make best use of natural light. ......

9. **Do you think the tips in the notice are good? Do you use them already?**

   ----

10. **Write another tip for the notice.**

Class bonus
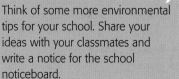

Think of some more environmental tips for your school. Share your ideas with your classmates and write a notice for the school noticeboard.

B Write down the number!

1 Look at the noticeboard. Complete the sentences with the correct numbers.

a Advertisements ...... and ...... are for things you can buy.

b Advertisements ...... and ...... are for things you can rent.

Learning tip

Sometimes you will be able to work out the meaning of a word you have never seen before because it looks similar to another English word you already know. For example, if you know the verb *alter*, you can work out from the context that *alterations* is the noun formed from this verb.

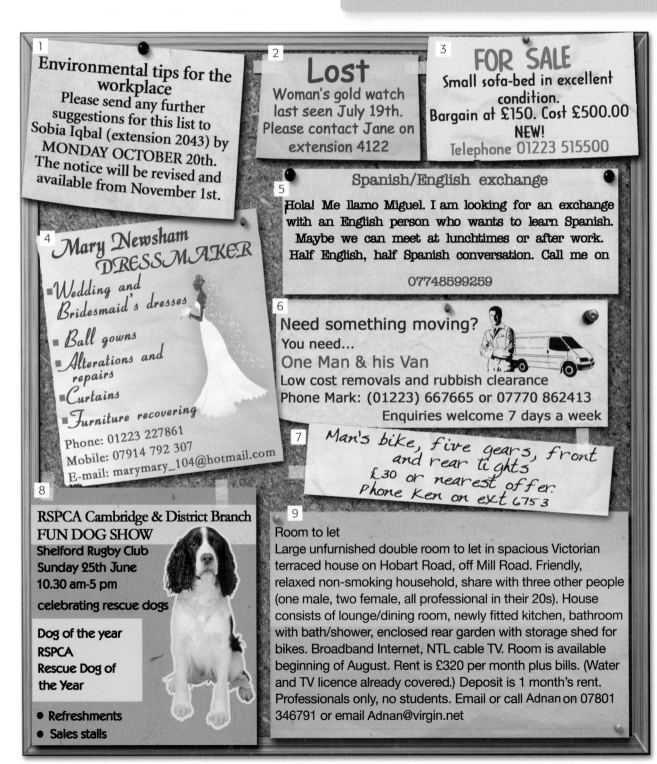

1
Environmental tips for the workplace
Please send any further suggestions for this list to Sobia Iqbal (extension 2043) by MONDAY OCTOBER 20th. The notice will be revised and available from November 1st.

2
Lost
Woman's gold watch last seen July 19th. Please contact Jane on extension 4122

3
FOR SALE
Small sofa-bed in excellent condition.
Bargain at £150. Cost £500.00 NEW!
Telephone 01223 515500

4
Mary Newsham
DRESSMAKER
▪ Wedding and Bridesmaid's dresses
▪ Ball gowns
▪ Alterations and repairs
▪ Curtains
▪ Furniture recovering
Phone: 01223 227861
Mobile: 07914 792 307
E-mail: marymary_104@hotmail.com

5
Spanish/English exchange
Hola! Me llamo Miguel. I am looking for an exchange with an English person who wants to learn Spanish. Maybe we can meet at lunchtimes or after work. Half English, half Spanish conversation. Call me on
07748599259

6
Need something moving?
You need...
One Man & his Van
Low cost removals and rubbish clearance
Phone Mark: (01223) 667665 or 07770 862413
Enquiries welcome 7 days a week

7
Man's bike, five gears, front and rear lights
£30 or nearest offer.
Phone Ken on ext 6753

8
RSPCA Cambridge & District Branch
FUN DOG SHOW
Shelford Rugby Club
Sunday 25th June
10.30 am-5 pm
celebrating rescue dogs

Dog of the year
RSPCA
Rescue Dog of the Year

● Refreshments
● Sales stalls

9
Room to let
Large unfurnished double room to let in spacious Victorian terraced house on Hobart Road, off Mill Road. Friendly, relaxed non-smoking household, share with three other people (one male, two female, all professional in their 20s). House consists of lounge/dining room, newly fitted kitchen, bathroom with bath/shower, enclosed rear garden with storage shed for bikes. Broadband Internet, NTL cable TV. Room is available beginning of August. Rent is £320 per month plus bills. (Water and TV licence already covered.) Deposit is 1 month's rent. Professionals only, no students. Email or call Adnan on 07801 346791 or email Adnan@virgin.net

2 Some people are interested in the advertisements. Scan the advertisements and find the answers to these questions.

1 What's the last date for sending tips?
   October 20th

2 You've found a gold watch. What extension number should you phone?
   ----

3 How much does the sofa-bed cost?
   ----

4 Will the dressmaker repair your trousers?
   ----

5 What's the Spanish boy's mobile number?
   ----

6 Will the man with the van move furniture?
   ----

7 How many gears does the bike have?
   ----

8 Where's the dog show?

Did you know …?

The RSPCA (Royal Society for the Prevention of Cruelty to Animals) was founded in 1824. Today there are more than seven million dogs in Britain and almost as many cats. Some of these are abandoned by their owners and have to be rescued by the RSPCA.

3 Andrés needs to leave the flat where he's living. Which advertisement will interest him most?

----

4 Skim the advertisement which interests Andrés. Do you think the room and house seem nice?

----

5 Look at the advertisement Andrés is interested in again. Find words which are related to the words a–e below. Then answer the questions with yes (Y) or no (N).

a furniture _____*unfurnished*_____
   Is there any furniture in the room? __N__

b space ----------------------------------
   Is there lots of space in the house? _____

c smoke ----------------------------------
   Can you smoke in this house? _____

d store ----------------------------------
   Is there somewhere you can store your bike? _____

e begin ----------------------------------
   Can you move in at the end of July? _____

6 Andrés would like to see the room. Scan the advertisement and answer these questions.

a Who does he have to contact?
   ----

b How much does the rent cost a month?
   ----

c Are bills included in the rent?
   ----

d What else will he have to pay when he moves in?
   ----

7 Andrés decides to take the room, but he doesn't have any furniture. Which other advertisements might interest him? Why?

   Advertisement 3 might interest him because

E ✗ tra practice

Where can you find advertisements in English in your town/city or country? Is there an English-language newspaper, for example? Find an advertisement for something that interests you.

Can-do checklist

Tick what you can do.

	Can do	Need more practice
I can scan advertisements and find information.	✔	
I can understand a list of tips.		✔
I can skim advertisements and decide if they are useful.	✔	

Unit 16
I'm working nights

Get ready to read

- Look at the pictures. These people all work in a hotel. What are their jobs? Match the words with the pictures.

  chambermaid [e]   chef ☐   porter ☐   receptionist ☐   waiter ☐

- Would you like to work during the night? Why? / Why not?

  <u>I'd like / I wouldn't like to work</u>
  <u>during the night because</u>

a   b   c   d   e

go to Useful language p. 86

A What does the job involve?

1 Claudio hears that there is a porter's job available at a local hotel. He does not really know what porters do, so he asks a friend. Think of three things that porters do.

----

2 Claudio looks on the Internet. He finds this information on a website about hotel and catering jobs. Skim the webpage. How many different types of hotel porter are there?

----

3 Look at the webpage again. Answer these questions.

a Which other people does the webpage mention?

----

b Are different words sometimes used for the same group of people?

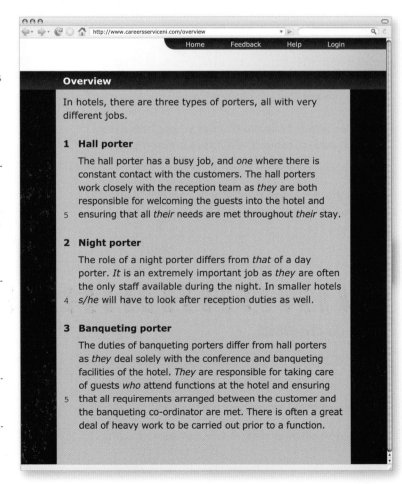

http://www.careersserviceni.com/overview

Home   Feedback   Help   Login

Overview

In hotels, there are three types of porters, all with very different jobs.

1 Hall porter

The hall porter has a busy job, and *one* where there is constant contact with the customers. The hall porters work closely with the reception team as *they* are both responsible for welcoming the guests into the hotel and
5 ensuring that all *their* needs are met throughout *their* stay.

2 Night porter

The role of a night porter differs from *that* of a day porter. *It* is an extremely important job as *they* are often the only staff available during the night. In smaller hotels
4 *s/he* will have to look after reception duties as well.

3 Banqueting porter

The duties of banqueting porters differ from hall porters as *they* deal solely with the conference and banqueting facilities of the hotel. *They* are responsible for taking care of guests *who* attend functions at the hotel and ensuring
5 that all requirements arranged between the customer and the banqueting co-ordinator are met. There is often a great deal of heavy work to be carried out prior to a function.

Learning tip

Some texts are hard to understand because they contain a lot of long sentences. Understanding who and what pronouns and possessive adjectives refer to can help you understand long sentences.

4 Look carefully at the first paragraph. What do the words in *italics* refer to? Circle the correct option.

a one (line 1)
  ① a job
  2 a hall porter
b they (line 3)
  1 hall porters
  2 hall porters and the reception team
c their (line 5)
  1 the hotel porters'
  2 the guests'
d their (line 5)
  1 the hotel porters'
  2 the guests'

5 What do these words in *italics* in the other two paragraphs refer to? Write your answers.

a that (paragraph 2, line 1)
  ....the role...........
b It (paragraph 2, line 2)
  ----
c they (paragraph 2, line 2)
  ----
d s/he (paragraph 2, line 4)
  ----
e they (paragraph 3, line 2)
  ----
f They (paragraph 3, line 3)
  ----
g who (paragraph 3, line 4)

Focus on ...
ing forms

We use the *ing* form of the verb after some prepositions. For example:
She's good at speaking to customers. He's thinking of becoming a chef.
We also use the *ing* form after *(be) responsible for.*

Which of the porters is responsible for these duties? Complete the sentences.
a The .... is responsible for welcoming guests into the hotel.
b The .... is responsible for ensuring that guests' needs are met.
c The .... is responsible for taking care of guests who attend functions.
d The .... is responsible for ensuring that all requirements arranged between the customer and the banqueting co-ordinator are met.

Complete these sentences about other duties in the hotel.
e The chef is responsible for .... the meals.
f The chambermaid is responsible for .... the rooms.
g The receptionist is responsible for .... guests in.
h The waiter is responsible for .... the meals.

6 The website also includes a list of each porter's duties. Read the lists and match the duties with the job titles in the Overview (page 76).

List A contains the *hall porter's / night porter's / banqueting porter's* duties.
List B contains the *hall porter's / night porter's / banqueting porter's* duties.

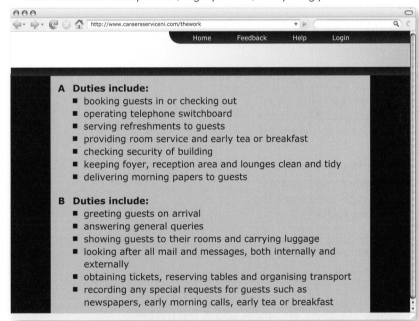

http://www.careersserviceni.com/thework

Home   Feedback   Help   Login

A Duties include:
- booking guests in or checking out
- operating telephone switchboard
- serving refreshments to guests
- providing room service and early tea or breakfast
- checking security of building
- keeping foyer, reception area and lounges clean and tidy
- delivering morning papers to guests

B Duties include:
- greeting guests on arrival
- answering general queries
- showing guests to their rooms and carrying luggage
- looking after all mail and messages, both internally and externally
- obtaining tickets, reserving tables and organising transport
- recording any special requests for guests such as newspapers, early morning calls, early tea or breakfast

7 Claudio would prefer to be a night porter so that he can study during the day. Which of the three jobs would you prefer?

I'd prefer to be a ---

E**X**tra practice

Claudio found out about porters' jobs on this website www/careersserviceni.com. Look on the website and read about the role of another hotel worker.

B A reminder for everyone

1 Look at the memo. Answer these questions.

a Who is it from?

   ----

b Who is it to?

Did you know …?

cc is an abbreviation for 'carbon copy'. It is used on a letter, email or memo to show that you are sending a copy to other people.

2 Look at the first paragraph. What is the topic of this paragraph? Tick ✓ the correct option. What do you think the word *shift* means?

a   duties during the evening shift ☐

b   new duties ☐

c   a reminder for everyone ☐

3 Look at the other three paragraphs. What is the topic of each paragraph?

4 Who should read each paragraph – all porters or porters who work the evening shift?

paragraph 1 --

paragraph 2 --

paragraph 3 --

paragraph 4 --

5 Complete these sentences about the porters.

a   They must --

b   They mustn't --

MEMO

To: All porters

From: Raquel Haines
cc: Paul Dawson
           Philippe Henry

Date: 6th December 2007

1   I have attached a list of duties that should be completed during the evening shift. The duties listed are not new. However, they are not always carried out by each porter, so it is a reminder for everyone.

2   I would also like to remind you that picking up litter needs to be improved. A sweep of the car parks and paths for litter must be carried out in the morning and afternoon before dark.

3   When each porter finishes his duties at the end of his shift, please ensure that you return all porters' keys to the KEY CUPBOARD. DO NOT LEAVE THEM at reception.

4   Finally, as you know, all staff should park in the staff car park and not use the guests' car park. I know this is a constant problem. However I expect you all to park in the staff car park and set an example.

If any of you require clarification, please ask.

Focus on …
pronouns

Find these pronouns in paragraph 1 of the memo. Who or what do they refer to?

a   I   ------------------------------

b   that   ------------------------------

c   they   ------------------------------

d   it   ------------------------------

Underline any pronouns in the rest of the memo. Who or what do they refer to?

6 Look at the list of duties which Raquel attached to her memo. Which duty did she mention in the memo? <u>Underline</u> this duty.

Daily

Before it gets dark: check paths and car parks for litter.

Check the newspapers in the lounge. Fold carefully, and place on table inside entrance.

Tidy the umbrellas and distribute around the hotel.

Check the fires on a regular basis and ensure the baskets are fully stocked with logs.

Check the main house and garden for tea trays.

Class bonus

Choose one of the duties in Exercise 6. Mime the action to a partner. Say what your partner is doing.

7 Look at the pictures. Which two duties has the porter on the evening shift not yet carried out? Write sentences.

He hasn't

1

2

3

4

5

6

8 There is one extra picture. Write another duty for Raquel's list.

Can-do checklist

Tick what you can do.

	Can do	Need more practice
I can work out who and what pronouns and possessive adjectives refer to.		
I can find out about the duties of a job.		
I can understand a memo.		
I can identify duties that have not been carried out.		

Review 2
Units 12–16

A Are these statements true (T) or false (F)?

1 Other words in a text can often help you to work out the meaning of an unknown word. ...... (Unit 12)

2 When you choose a reader, make sure it has lots of words that you do not know. ...... (Unit 13)

3 You should always read exam instructions carefully. ...... (Unit 14)

4 You should always read to the end of a text before you look for a particular piece of information. ...... (Unit 15)

5 Working out who or what pronouns and possessive adjectives refer to in a text is not a good use of your time. ...... (Unit 16)

B Now read the *Learning tips* for Units 12–16 on pages 90–91. Do you want to change any of your answers in Exercise A?

C Skim the five texts on these pages. Decide which text these people would read. Write the letter of the text in the box.

6 someone who is thinking about taking the KET exam ☐

7 someone who is planning a holiday ☐

8 someone who wants to read for pleasure ☐

9 someone who is thinking about changing jobs ☐

10 someone who is not going to be working at their desk ☐

Text A

| CAMBRIDGE | **English Readers** | | Beginner/ Elementary |

Liz studies and teaches archaeology in Athens. She works hard and needs a holiday, so she goes to the beautiful and peaceful island of Sifnos. But the peace does not last long. When a mysterious yacht arrives, one of the local men dies, and Liz becomes involved with some very dangerous people.

Cambridge English Readers is an exciting series of original fiction, specially written for learners of English. Graded into seven levels – from starter to advanced – the stories in this series provide easy and enjoyable reading on a wide range of contemporary topics and themes.

Visit the Cambridge English Readers website for free resources, including a worksheet for this title: www.cambridge.org/elt/readers

Text B

Examination preparation

We provide preparation for the following General English examinations: University of Cambridge Examinations and Trinity College examinations.

Preparation Classes

Examination candidates take part in General English classes every morning. There are special examination preparation classes in the afternoons.

In the morning classes, you study and practise all aspects of English – reading, writing, listening, speaking, grammar, vocabulary, etc. The aim of these lessons is to improve your general level of English. You have two different teachers and each lesson lasts 75 minutes. There is a 30-minute break between the two lessons.

You will have Exam Preparation classes on four afternoons a week (you are free on Wednesday afternoons). In these classes, you practise the specific types of questions found in the exams. The first lesson is devoted to Listening & Speaking, and the second lesson to Reading & Writing. Both lessons last for an hour, and there is a 15-minute break between them. You will have the same teacher for each lesson.

Preparation classes for Cambridge Exams start in January, March and September, and last for eight weeks. Please check our website for course dates, exam dates and dates of registration for the exam. Note that the cost of the examinations may change. Ask the school for up-to-date information about the fees.

Text C

> Hotel receptionists perform one of the
> most vital roles in the hotel industry
> as *they* are the first point of contact a
> customer has with the hotel.
> 5 Small hotels may only employ one or two
> receptionists, whereas larger *ones* may
> have a team of eight or nine.
> Duties can roughly be divided into 'front'
> – welcoming and registering guests,
> 10 dealing with *their* queries – and 'back'
> – working behind the scenes. In a small
> hotel, however, *these* may include both
> types of work.

Text D

How to record a personal greeting on your phone extension

- Enter your extension number and your password.
- Select option 6.
- Dial 1 to record your personal greeting.
- Your personal greeting should be changed daily and contain the following information.
  a Your name.
  b The day and date.
  c Your movements for that day.
  d If appropriate, an alternative extension number of a colleague who may be able to assist if the call is urgent.
  e Ask the caller to leave a message.
  f Details of when you will be able to return the call.

Text E

Ski apartment

Booking now for next winter

Comfortable 3-bedroom ski apartment sleeps up to 7. Open fire, DVD player, dishwasher, washing machine, 2 bathrooms. Balcony views to the mountains. Ski lifts, restaurants and shops within walking distance.

Bansko is both a modern winter sports centre and a working town. It offers a true alternative to the Alps at a fraction of the price.

For further information and availability, please call Jania 01492 513109

D Answer these questions about Text A. Write one, two, three or four words only.

11 What kind of boat is mentioned in the blurb?
----
12 A man dies. Where is he from? ----------------------------
13 Which word has the same meaning as 'fiction'?
----
14 Which two words explain the meaning of 'original'?

E You want to take the KET exam. A friend tells you about the courses at his school. Read Text B. Are your friend's sentences true (T) or false (F)?

15 You take exam preparation classes in the morning. ......
16 There are no lessons on Wednesday afternoons. ......
17 You have one teacher in the morning and a different one in the afternoon. ......
18 The school runs three exam preparation courses each year. ......

F Read Text C. What do the words in *italics* refer to? Write one or two words.

19 they (line 3) ----------------------------
20 ones (line 6) ----------------------------
21 their (line 10) ----------------------------
22 these (line 12) ----------------------------

G Read Text D. Here are your notes for recording your personal message. Match four of the points (a–f) with the notes. Write the letters in the boxes.

23 Please leave a message when you hear the bleep. □

24 I will call you back tomorrow morning (Thursday the 19th). □

25 I won't be at my desk between 3 and 5.30pm. □

26 You have reached the personal voicemail of Mirella Tonioli. I'm sorry I'm not here to take your call. □

H Read Text E. You are interested in renting this apartment for yourself and five friends. Answer these questions. Write one word only.

27 Is the apartment big enough for you? ----------------------
28 Do you need a car to get to the skiing area? ----------------------
29 Where is the apartment exactly? ----------------------
30 Are you likely to find a cheaper apartment in the Alps?

Appendix 1
Useful language

This section contains a list of words which are important for carrying out the reading exercises for each unit. You can use the list in three ways.

1 You can look at the list before you begin the unit and make sure that you understand the meaning of the words by looking them up in a dictionary.
2 You can look at the list before you begin the unit, but try and work out the meaning of the words when you meet them in the unit.
3 You can look at the list when you have completed the unit and check that you understand the words.

When you start using the book, you may prefer to use the list in the first way. However, you will find each word in one of the texts, and the context – the words around the unknown word – will help you to work out its meaning. As you develop your reading skills, you will probably realise that it is not necessary to look at the list before you begin the unit. You may already know some of the words; you will be able to work out others from the text or the task.

Each list is a record of the vocabulary of the unit. You can use it as a checklist when you have completed the unit. There is space after each word to write a translation in your own language or an English expression using the word. Mark each word that you understand and can use with a highlighter pen.

There is also space below the wordlist for you to write other words from the unit which are important to you. Look at *Appendix 3* for ideas on what to record for each word.

Unit 1
Reading A
airport *noun* --
arrivals *noun* --
passport *noun* --
baggage *noun* --
exit *noun* --
Customs *noun* --

Reading B
train *noun* --
journey *noun* --
city centre *noun* --
ticket *noun* --
taxi *noun* --
wheelchair *noun* --
underground *noun* --
taxi rank *noun* --
station *noun* --

Unit 2
Reading A
menu *noun* --
leaflet *noun* --
bill *noun* --
breakfast *noun* --
buffet *noun* --
free *adjective* --
weekends *noun* --
book *verb* --
reception *noun* --
check in *verb* --

Reading B
appetisers *noun* --
mains *noun* --
vegetarian *adjective and noun* --

Unit 3

Reading A

specialist shop *noun* _____
department store *noun* _____
supermarket *noun* _____
accessories *noun* _____
cosmetics *noun* _____
footwear *noun* _____
childrenswear *noun* _____
luggage *noun* _____
gadgets and games *noun* _____
ground floor *noun* _____
first floor *noun* _____
second floor *noun* _____
_____
_____
_____

Reading B

escalator *noun* _____
exit *noun* _____
fitting room *noun* _____
ordering service *noun* _____
emergency *noun* _____
tax-free shopping *noun* _____
non-EC resident *noun* _____
exclude *verb* _____
sale *noun* _____
half price *adjective* _____
best-selling *adjective* _____
lift *noun* _____
out of order *expression* _____
cheque *noun* _____
credit card *noun* _____
mind *verb* _____
cash *noun* _____
_____
_____
_____

Unit 4

Reading A

currency exchange *noun* _____
ATM (automated teller machine) *noun* _____
debit card *noun* _____
credit card *noun* _____
exchange rate *noun* _____
cash *noun* _____
travellers cheques *noun* _____
commission *noun* _____
receipt *noun* _____
_____
_____
_____

Reading B

PIN (personal identification number) *noun* _____
key *noun* _____
_____
_____
_____
_____

Unit 5

Reading A

balcony *noun* _____
overlook *verb* _____
facilities *noun* _____
fittings *noun* _____
services *noun* _____
safe deposit box *noun* _____
_____
_____
_____

Reading B

budget hotel *noun* _____
laundry service *noun* _____
rates *noun* _____
_____
_____
_____

Unit 6

Reading A

chemist's *noun* _____
tablets *noun* _____
medication *noun* _____
soap *noun* _____
shampoo *noun* _____
advice *noun* _____
cosmetics _____
dental products *noun* _____
(healthy) food *noun* _____
health care *noun* _____
toiletries *noun* _____
_____
_____
_____

Reading B

headache *noun* _____

cold *noun* _____

flu *noun* _____

swallow *verb* _____

exceed *verb* _____

(blocked) nose *noun* _____

spray *noun* _____

invert *verb* _____

upright *adjective* _____

nostril *noun* _____

squeeze *noun* _____

_____

_____

_____

Unit 7
Reading A

many happy returns *exclamation* _____

with deepest sympathy *expression* _____

get better soon *expression* _____

good luck *exclamation* _____

congratulations *exclamation* _____

colleague *noun* _____

_____

_____

_____

Reading B

email *noun* _____

note *noun* _____

postcard *noun* _____

text message *noun* _____

tenpin bowling *noun* _____

fantasy *noun* _____

urgent *adjective* _____

_____

_____

_____

Unit 8
Reading A

park *verb* _____

ride *verb* _____

ring road *noun* _____

architecture *noun* _____

_____

_____

_____

Reading B

machine *noun* _____

pay *verb* _____

display *verb* _____

vehicle *noun* _____

charges *noun* _____

penalty charge *noun* _____

_____

_____

_____

Unit 9
Reading A

accommodation *noun* _____

excursion *noun* _____

discount *noun* _____

souvenir *noun* _____

_____

_____

_____

Reading B

attraction *noun* _____

aquarium *noun* _____

seal *noun* _____

entrance fee *noun* _____

harbour *noun* _____

double-decker coach *noun* _____

cable car *noun* _____

_____

_____

_____

Unit 10
Reading A

doctor *noun* _____

nurse *noun* _____

patient *noun* _____

receptionist *noun* _____

appointment *noun* _____

register *verb* _____

delay *noun* _____

medical record *noun* _____

_____

_____

_____

Reading B

operation *noun* _____

pregnancy *noun* _____

disability *noun* _____

prescription *noun* _____

allergy *noun* _____

medication *noun* _____

heart attack *noun* _____

stroke *noun* _____

_____

_____

_____

Unit 11
Reading A

comedy *noun* _____

fantasy *noun* _____

horror *noun* _____

romance *noun* _____

thriller *noun* _____

cartoon *noun* _____

chat show *noun* _____

documentary *noun* _____

drama *noun* _____

game show *noun* _____

quiz show *noun* _____

sitcom *noun* _____

soap opera *noun* _____

_____

_____

_____

Reading B

artwork *noun* _____

animation *noun* _____

casting *noun* _____

performances *noun* _____

_____

_____

_____

Unit 12
Reading A

dream *noun and verb* _____

achieve *verb* _____

fully recognised *adjective* _____

range *adjective* _____

dedicated *adjective* _____

enrol *verb* _____

qualified *adjective* _____

_____

_____

_____

Reading B

full-time *adjective* _____

part-time *adjective* _____

grammatical correctness *noun* _____

fee *noun* _____

_____

_____

_____

Unit 13
Reading A

title *noun* _____

cover *noun* _____

blurb *noun* _____

graded reader *noun* _____

murder mystery *noun* _____

thriller *noun* _____

science fiction *noun* _____

romance *noun* _____

_____

_____

_____

Reading B

chapter *noun* _____

_____

_____

_____

Unit 14
Reading A

grade *noun* _____

pass *noun* _____

fail *noun* _____

results slip *noun* _____

skill *noun* _____

answer sheet *noun* _____

transfer *verb* _____

candidate *noun* _____

examiner *noun* _____

_____

_____

_____

Reading B

signature *noun* _____

_____

_____

_____

Unit 15

Reading A

cartridge *noun* ....
fax machine *noun* ....
heater *noun* ....
mug *noun* ....
paper clip *noun* ....
plastic wallet *noun* ....
post-it note *noun* ....
printer *noun* ....
rubber band *noun* ....
scrap paper *noun* ....
....
....
....
....

Reading B

sofa-bed *noun* ....
dressmaker *noun* ....
removals *noun* ....
gears *noun* ....
....
....
....

Unit 16

Reading A

chambermaid *noun* ....
chef *noun* ....
porter *noun* ....
receptionist *noun* ....
waiter *noun* ....
banqueting porter *noun* ....
responsible *adjective* ....
function *noun* ....
requirement *noun* ....
....
....
....

Reading B

shift *noun* ....
sweep *verb* ....
clarification *noun* ....
....
....
....

Appendix 2
Learning tips

Each unit of this book contains one *Learning tip*. However, this does not mean that this *Learning tip* is useful in only that particular unit. Most *Learning tips* can be used in several different units. Here are all the *Learning tips* in the book. Each one is under its unit heading and you will also find a list of the types of text you read in that unit.

When you have completed a unit, decide which text you used the *Learning tip* with (this could be more than one text type). In addition, look at the other *Learning tips* and decide if you also used any of those tips in the unit you have just finished. Make a note of the unit name and number and the text type on the empty lines. In this way, you can keep a record of the reading strategies that you are developing.

Unit 1 We're here!

Learning tip

If you speak a European language, some English words may look similar to words in your language. This will help you to understand the meaning of words you do not know. For example:
arrivals – *arrivi* (Italian)
passport – *pasaporte* (Spanish)
baggage – *bagages* (French)
passenger – *passageiro* (Portuguese)
toilet – *toaleta* (Polish)

A signs ☐
B website ☐
   map ☐
   ticket ☐
   timetable ☐

Which other units have you used this *Learning tip* in?

Unit 2 What can I eat?

Learning tip

When you read, it is not necessary to understand every word in the text. You only need to understand the parts of the text which contain the information you are looking for.

A hotel leaflet ☐
B menu ☐

Which other units have you used this *Learning tip* in?

Unit 3 Where will I find it?

Learning tip

Scanning is when we read a text quickly to find a particular piece of information. We do not read every word. We stop reading when we find the information we want.

A store guide ☐
B shop signs ☐

Which other units have you used this *Learning tip* in?

Unit**4** Can I get money here?

Learning tip

Prepare yourself for reading a text by thinking about the topic in your own language. This will help you to predict the content of the English text and work out the meaning of any unknown words.

A Currency Exchange leaflet ☐
B ATM machine instructions ☐

Which other units have you used this *Learning tip* in?

Unit**5** Somewhere to stay

Learning tip

Skimming is when we read a text quickly to find out what it is about or to get a general idea. We do not read every word. We get the main idea and we don't pay attention to details. (See also *Learning tip* in Unit 6.)

A hotel website ☐
B hotel website ☐

Which other units have you used this *Learning tip* in?

Unit**6** Is this what I need?

Learning tip

We often skim a text to find the part of the text which is most useful/important to us. We read the important part slowly, and we probably read some words and sentences more than once in order to understand the details. It is particularly important to read instructions carefully. (See also *Learning tip* in Unit 5.)

A labels on bottles and packets ☐
     bill ☐
B instructions on medication ☐

Which other units have you used this *Learning tip* in?

Unit**7** Who's it from?

Learning tip

When we read a text, we want to understand the writer's message. To do this, we read silently. In real life, we sometimes read aloud – for example, we might read out something interesting from a newspaper to a friend. Reading aloud does not help you to understand the message, but it helps you to practise the language.

A greetings cards ☐
B email ☐
     text message ☐
     note ☐
     postcard ☐

Which other units have you used this *Learning tip* in?

Unit 8 Where can we park?

Learning tip

As you read, try to work out the meaning of unknown words. Find other words in the text which might help you with the meaning of the word you do not know. Perhaps some other words in the text have the same meaning – or the opposite meaning. Only use a dictionary to check your guesses.

a leaflet about parking ☐
b parking machine notice ☐

Which other units have you used this *Learning tip* in?

Unit 9 Let's go there

Learning tip

Your knowledge of grammar will not help you with the meaning of unknown words. But it will help you to decide whether words are nouns, verbs, etc. This will help you to link words in sentences and to read words in groups.

a Tourist Information leaflet ☐
b leaflets for attractions ☐

Which other units have you used this *Learning tip* in?

Unit 10 I'd like to register

Learning tip

When you need to read a difficult text, you will read some words and sentences very carefully. In order to understand difficult parts of texts, it is a good idea to try and put the sentences of the text into your own words.

A leaflet about medical practice ☐
B application form ☐

Which other units have you used this *Learning tip* in?

Unit 11 What's on tonight?

Learning tip

You can use either a dictionary with English and your language or a dictionary which has definitions in English. The main advantage of using a dictionary which has definitions in English is that you are working in English all the time. These dictionaries also explain the different meanings that one word can have, and they give lots of examples of how words are used.

A TV guide ☐
B film review ☐

Which other units have you used this *Learning tip* in?

Unit 12 This school sounds good!

Learning tip

It is important to try and guess the meaning of words that you do not know. Usually the context (the rest of the text) will help you decide on a possible meaning for them. Don't use a dictionary to find out the meaning of every unknown word, as this takes too long and also interrupts your reading. Only use a dictionary to check your guesses.

A language school website ☐
B language school website ☐

Which other units have you used this *Learning tip* in?

Unit 13 I've chosen this one!

Learning tip

Extensive reading – reading stories – should be a pleasure! Do not choose a reader with too many difficult words and structures. Read part of the first chapter before you buy or borrow a book – and find out if it's the right level for you. Try to read whole sections – pages, chapters, etc. – without stopping. Aim to get a general overall understanding of the story. When you have done this, you can go back and read the text again more slowly and carefully if you need to.

A book covers ☐
B part of a chapter ☐

Which other units have you used this *Learning tip* in?

Unit 14 Use a pencil!

Learning tip

Make sure you read exam instructions very carefully. As well as telling you what to do, exam instructions sometimes give you important information about the topic. Always look at examples. They show you what to do. In matching tasks, they also show which answer cannot be used again.

A exam description ☐
B exam paper ☐

Which other units have you used this *Learning tip* in?

Unit 15 It's on the noticeboard

Learning tip

Sometimes you will be able to work out the meaning of a word you have never seen before because it looks similar to another English word you already know. For example, if you know the verb *alter*, you can work out from the context that *alterations* is the noun formed from this verb.

A workplace notice ☐
B advertisements ☐

Which other units have you used this *Learning tip* in?

Unit 16 I'm working nights

> ### Learning tip
>
> Some texts are hard to understand because they contain a lot of long sentences. Understanding who and what pronouns and possessive adjectives refer to can help you understand long sentences.

A jobs website ☐
B memo ☐
attachment ☐

Which other units have you used this *Learning tip* in?

Appendix 3
Using a dictionary

What kind of dictionary should I use?

If possible, you should use two dictionaries: a good bilingual dictionary (in both your own language and with English translations) and a good monolingual dictionary (English words with English definitions). A monolingual dictionary may give you more information about a word or phrase; in addition, it is a good idea for you to work in English as much as possible. The examples on these pages are from the *Cambridge Essential English Dictionary*.

What information can I find in a dictionary?

The most common reason for looking a word up in a dictionary is to find out its meaning. However, a dictionary can also give you a lot of other information about a word. The *Cambridge Essential English Dictionary*, for example, can give up to six types of information before the meaning of the word and four further types of information after it. These examples are all from Unit 1.

1   the main form of the word

> In blue you will see the main form of the word.

> **airport** /ˈeəpɔːt/ *noun*
> **a place where aeroplanes take off and land**

2   the pronunciation of the word

> These symbols show you how to say the word.

> **city** /ˈsɪti/ *noun (plural* **cities)**
> **a large town**

3   its part of speech

> This tells you what part of speech – noun, verb, adjective, etc. – a word is.

> **taxi** /ˈtæksi/ *noun*
> **a car with a driver who you pay to take you somewhere:** *I'll take a taxi to the airport.*

4 whether the word is only used in British English (UK) or American English (US)

> *UK* means that a word is only used in British English; *US* means that a word is used only in American English.

centre *UK* (*US* **center**) /'sentə^r/ *noun*
1 the middle point or part of something: *Cars are not allowed in the town centre.*
2 a building used for a particular activity: *a health centre*
3 **be the centre of attention** to get more attention than anyone else

5 any special grammatical features of the word

baggage /'bægɪdʒ/ *noun* [no plural]
all the cases and bags that you take with you when you travel

> **[no plural]** shows that you cannot add '*s*' to this noun to make it plural.

6 irregular past tense forms, plural nouns, and comparatives/superlatives

> Plurals which are not regular are shown.

bus /bʌs/ *noun* (*plural* **buses**)
a large vehicle that carries passengers by road, usually along a fixed route: *a school bus*

7 the meaning of the word

customs /'kʌstəmz/ *noun* [no plural]
the place where your bags are examined when you are going into a country

> The definition tells you what the word means.

8 an illustration of the word

trolley

> These illustrations shows you what the word means.

trolley /'trɒli/ *noun UK* (*plural* **trolleys**)
a metal structure on wheels that is used for carrying things: *a luggage trolley*

9 example phrases or sentences

including /ɪn'kluːdɪŋ/ *preposition*
used to show that someone or something is part of something larger: *It's £24.99, including postage and packing.* ⊃Opposite **excluding**

> An example (in *italics*) can show you how a word is used in a sentence.

10 other words this word goes with (collocations)

> **arrive** /əˈraɪv/ *verb* (*present participle* **arriving**, *past* **arrived**)
> to get to a place: *We **arrived in** Paris at midday.* ○ *I was the last to **arrive at** the station.* ↄOpposite **leave**

Words in **bold** in an example show you which words are often used together.

11 the opposite of the word (where it exists)

> **cheap** /tʃiːp/ *adj*
> not expensive, or costing less than usual: *a cheap flight* ↄOpposite **expensive**

If the word has an opposite, this is shown at the end.

How should I use my dictionary?

1 At the top of each page in the *Cambridge Essential English Dictionary*, there is a word in **bold** black type. You can use this word to help you find the word you are looking for quickly. The word in the top left corner of the left page is the first word on this page; the word in the top right corner of the right page is the last word on this page. If you are looking for the word **main**, it will be between the two words **mail** and **map** (top right corner of the right page).

mail	192
mail² /meɪl/ *verb US* to send a letter or parcel or email something: *Could you **mail** it to me?* **mailbox** /ˈmeɪlbɒks/ *noun US* **1** a small box outside your home where letters are put **2** (*UK* **post box**) a large, metal container in a public place where you can post letters **main** /meɪn/ *adj* most important or largest: *Our main problem is lack of money.* ○ *The main airport is 15 miles from the capital.* **mainly** /ˈmeɪnli/ *adv* mostly: *The people are mainly French*	**2 make someone do something** to force someone to do something: *You can't make me go.* **3 make someone/something happy/ sad/difficult, etc** to cause someone or something to become happy, sad, difficult, etc: *You've made me very happy.* **4** If you make an amount of money, you earn it: *He makes £20,000 a year.* **5** If two or more numbers make a particular amount, that is the amount when they are added together: *That makes $40 altogether.* **6 make the bed** to make the sheets

	193	map
insect) bites you **male¹** /meɪl/ *adj* belonging to or relating to the sex that cannot have babies: *a male colleague* ↄOpposite **female** **male²** /meɪl/ *noun* a male person or animal **mall** /mɔːl/ (*also* **shopping mall**) *noun* a large, covered shopping area **mammal** /ˈmæmᵊl/ *noun* an animal that drinks milk from its mother's body when it is young **man** /mæn/ *noun* (*plural* **men**) **1** an adult male human: *a young man*		**mankind** /mænˈkaɪnd/ *noun* [no plural] all people, considered as a group: *the history of mankind* **man-made** /ˌmænˈmeɪd/ *adj* not natural, but made by people: *man-made fibres* **manner** /ˈmænəʳ/ *noun* **1** the way in which a person talks and behaves with other people: *She has a very friendly manner.* **2** the way something happens or something is done: *They dealt with the problem in a very efficient manner.* **manners** /ˈmænəz/ *plural noun*

2 Each time you look up a word, you could use a highlighter pen to mark the word in your dictionary. When you return to a page with a highlighter mark, look at the word quickly and check that you remember its meaning.

> **existence** /ɪgˈzɪstᵊns/ *noun* [no plural]
> when something or someone exists: *The theatre company that we started is still **in existence** today.*
>
> **exit** /ˈeksɪt/ *noun*
> the door which you use to leave a public building or place: *a fire exit* ○ *an emergency exit*
>
> **expand** /ɪkˈspænd/ *verb*
> to get larger, or to make something get larger: *The company has expanded in recent years.*

3   A word in your dictionary may not be exactly the same
    as its form in the text you are reading. This is because
    the word in the text may be:

    a   an irregular form of a verb ending in -ed, -ing -s,
        e.g. *costs*

> **cost²** /kɒst/ *verb* (*present participle*
> **costing**, *past* **cost**)
> If something costs a particular
> amount of money, you have to pay
> that in order to buy or do it: *How
> much do these shoes cost?* ∘ ***It costs** $5
> to send the package by airmail.*

    b   a plural form of a noun, e.g. *citizens*

> **citizen** /ˈsɪtɪzən/ *noun*
> someone who lives in a particular
> town or city: *the citizens of Berlin*

    c   a comparative or superlative form of an adjective, e.g. *quickest*

> **quick** /kwɪk/ *adj*
> doing something fast or taking only
> a short time: *I tried to catch him but he
> was too quick for me.*

4   The words that are defined in the dictionary are called
    headwords. (In the *Cambridge Essential English Dictionary*,
    headwords are in blue.) Sometimes a headword can have more
    than one meaning. The first meaning in the dictionary is not
    always the one you want. Read through the different meanings
    and decide which one is correct in this context.

> **arrange** /əˈreɪndʒ/ *verb* (*present
> participle* **arranging**, *past* **arranged**)
> **1** to make plans for something to
> happen: *I've arranged a meeting with
> him.*
> **2** to put objects in a particular order
> or position: *Arrange the books
> alphabetically by author.*

5   Some words in your dictionary may have more than one headword.
    (Small numbers after the headword will indicate this.) This is because
    the word can be used as different parts of speech – for example, a
    noun and a verb. The part of speech of the unknown word should be
    clear from the context (the words around it).

> **underground¹** /ˈʌndəɡraʊnd/ *adj,
> adv*
> under the surface of the ground: *an
> animal that lives underground*
> **underground²** /ˈʌndəɡraʊnd/ *noun*
> UK
> a system of trains that is built under
> a city: *the London Underground*

When should I use my dictionary?

A dictionary is very useful when you are learning a foreign language. However, when
you are reading, do not use your dictionary too much. Using your dictionary will interrupt
your reading and slow you down. In your own language, you don't always understand
the meaning of every word; it is not necessary to understand everything in English either.

1   When you see an English word that you don't know, first try to guess the meaning
    of the word from its context (the words around it). You may find another word with
    a similar meaning, a word which means the opposite, or some words which actually
    explain the unknown word. Only use your dictionary to check your guess.

2   The only other time you should look a word up in your dictionary is if there are no
    clues in the text and you are sure the unknown word is important.